Toxic Parents The Ultimate Guide

Recognizing, Understanding and Recovering from Narcissistic Parents. This book includes: Emotionally Immature Parents, Narcissistic Mothers and Fathers

Dr. Theresa J.Covert

© Copyright 2020 - All rights reserved.

The content contained within this book may not be reproduced, duplicated or transmitted without direct written permission from the author or the publisher.

Under no circumstances will any blame or legal responsibility be held against the publisher, or author, for any damages, reparation, or monetary loss due to the information contained within this book; either directly or indirectly.

Legal Notice:

This book is copyright protected. This book is only for personal use. You cannot amend, distribute, sell, use, quote or paraphrase any part, or the content within this book, without the consent of the author or publisher.

Disclaimer Notice:

Please note the information contained within this document is for educational and entertainment purposes only. All effort has been executed to present accurate, up to date, and reliable, complete information. No warranties of any kind are declared or implied. Readers acknowledge that the author is not engaging in the rendering of legal, financial, medical or professional advice.

Table of Contents
Emotionally Immature Parents

Emotionally Immature parents 6

Introduction 7

Chapter 1   The consequences of Emotional Immaturity on Adult Children 12

Chapter 2   Understanding who is an Emotionally Immature Parent 19

Chapter 3   What do the affected children go through 28

Chapter 4   Different ways of being an Emotionally Immature Parent 39

Chapter 5   Behavioural patterns of Children with Emotionally Immature Parents 50

Chapter 6   Being an Internalizer 61

Chapter 7   The Dusk Before the Dawn 74

Chapter 8   Being Free From Emotionally Immature Parents 88

Chapter 9   Living Free of Roles and Responsibilities 96

Chapter 10   What is an Emotionally Mature person 108

Conclusion 117

Table of Contents
Narcissistic Fathers

Narcissistic Fathers 120

Introduction 121

Chapter 1 Who are narcissistic fathers? 125

Chapter 2 Signs of a narcissistic father 129

Chapter 3 The dark core of personality in narcissistic fathers 136

Chapter 4 Narcissistic fathers and their inability to love 141

Chapter 5 Weapons of a narcissist: How a narcissistic father controls... 145

Chapter 6 Narcissistic fathers and unhealthy family dynamics 152

Chapter 7 The scapegoat vs. the golden child 157

Chapter 8 The wounds of the scapegoated child...... 166

Chapter 9 Narcissistic fathers, their sons, and daughters 176

Chapter 10 The effects of paternal narcissism on children... 184

Chapter 11 Breaking free from a narcissistic father . 208

Chapter 12 Steps to healing and rewriting your story 214

Conclusion 227

Table of Contents
Narcissistic Mothers

Narcissistic Mothers 231

Introduction 232

Chapter 1 Narcissistic Personality Disorder 235

Chapter 2 Types of Narcissism 246

Chapter 3 How to Recognize A Narcissistic Mother 259

Chapter 4 Behaviors of a Narcissistic Mother 266

Chapter 5 The Signs That You Have a Narcissistic Mother 275

Chapter 6 Treatment for Children of Narcissistic Mothers 290

Chapter 7 Things Narcissistic Mothers Say for Mental Manipulation and Control 309

Chapter 8 Protection Tips 328

Chapter 9 Separating from a Narcissistic Mother 339

Chapter 10: How to HEAL from ABUSE! 343

Conclusion 354

Emotionally Immature parents

Overcoming Childhood Emotional Neglect due to Absent and Self Involved Parents

Dr. Theresa J. Covert

Introduction

We might be used to assuming that every grown up person is way more developed intellectually or more - *mature* than every child, but have you ever wondered what might happen if things were different? Maybe things are beginning to change with children and they could be turning out to be emotionally stronger than their fathers and mothers I know it could sound funny to you, but that's the science behind it. Things can change and our children can become more sensitive than us as parents. So, what do you do when that happens? You know what's more dangerous with an emotionally smarter and stronger child is that they may even end up having parents with weak emotional strength. How then do these parents with low emotional range and maturity interact with their children's advances? You know what might happen when such parents don't step up? Sooner or later, they end up as parents who don't show their children the emotional love and bond they need. Physical withdrawal is becoming more and more of a reality from both children and parents.

You see, when a parent ignores their children's emotional needs, it leads to a messy childhood. Your kids might end up being emotionally empty or desolate and what's more scary about this loneliness is that it will most likely cause a prolonged adverse effect on your child's choices when it comes to choosing relationships and life partners in adulthood. That's the point of this book; it will help you with a lot of things to aid your emotional growth with your children. It is a book that will tell you ways in which parents with weak emotional capacity, who are immature may cause major problems in their children's life, especially when you as a parent have children that are also emotionally unstable. This book tells you ways in which you can rebuild yourself and recover from that sinking feeling of torture and disorientation that comes along with having fathers and mothers who do not believe or share the idea of emotional closeness.

Parents who are emotionally unsteady are usually afraid of accurate psychological state and tug back at emotional proximity. Now, such parents turn towards management techniques that counteract all this. They now find thinking inwardly as unwelcoming, so they hardly ever admit to making mistakes or make an apology. Their immature state of mind makes them irregular and emotionally undependable, and undiscerning to the needs of their kids.

I have taken the time to create imaginable and understandable points that will help you know that as a parent, when you are weak emotional, you will have problems, especially when your kids have so much emotional needs. Children's books in today's society also reflect this phenomenon. Nowadays, the amount of children's stories that are about children who are left on their own and must help an animal in pain just because their parents are uncaring, inexperienced, or absent-minded, are on the increase. There are also other stories where the parents of the character are truly wicked and in such cases, the kids are left to their own devices, without the help of their parents. Such fairy tales have been in our lives so long and you know why? These stories have a lesson that helps so many children all over the world on ways to take care of themselves. Well, this kind of story tells us one thing: children have had immature parents for a very long time.

With this book, I believe you will get the answers to so many questions you have asked your friends or even other parents that seem to have a balanced life with their kids. You must be wondering why relating to some people in your family is annoying, irritating, painful and frustrating. Well, that's the point of this book; it helps you understand the idea of maturing when it comes to your emotions and relationships. This therefore helps you improve on your hopes of other people, and also allows you to connect with others without having these hurtful feelings..

There are psychotherapists who believe that when kids separate themselves emotionally from fathers and mothers who are toxic, they can bring back comfort and self-support to themselves. Now, have you ever wondered how this can be done? How to bring peace to yourself?. So many things are missing in the lives of immature parents and this causes a breakdown on their capacity to show love. I have learned these things and put it into this book which fills the gap, and sheds some light on the reasons why some parents do not have emotional maturity. This will help you recognize some traits in your kids and then you will learn to review yourself and the type of relationship you can have with them.

You need to know this now; when you comprehend why a parent is emotionally immature, it lets one get the true meaning of being lonely. The fact that a parent doesn't attend to a child's needs when it comes to emotions doesn't mean they hate the child. It is a problem they are battling within themselves. You will learn so many things and it begins with knowing that there are parents that can't change, so you will know that getting angry about it is a waste of time. As I mentioned, a parent who doesn't show emotional care to their children isn't a bad parent, they just don't know how to show it.

In addition, you will learn reasons why either or both parents lack these emotional traits in them. There are things you need to know and this book gives you that: it teaches you that you are not a shadow and your parents don't hate you. Trying to communicate with them is good but even if it doesn't turn out to be fruitful, it still doesn't mean they are bad people and it doesn't mean you are not a useful child.

Without much further ado, here are the things you stand to learn when you read this book:

You get to know why people who were raised by parents that are not emotionally mature are likely to feel detached emotionally.

You will discover the traits of parents who are not mature emotionally and recognize the kinds of problems that might come from having immature parents. It is useful for both parents and children of immature parents. As you read this book, you will learn about your parent's perplexing actions and their actions will begin to make sense. I have provided a list that will help you note the areas where your parents are lacking emotionally or where you are lacking emotionally as a parent. You need an understanding of these traits, and then you will get every reason why your parent stopped growing emotionally.

There are four kinds of parents who are not emotionally mature and in these books, you will know these types of parents and you will be able to detect the type of parenting style your parents used on you. One of these parenting styles may lead to self-hindering habits that kids may show just so they can get by with these kinds of four parents.

Chapter 1

The consequences of Emotional Immaturity on Adult Children

So the question is, how can a parent who isn't emotionally mature cause an adverse effect on their children even after they are grown?

Emotional solitude arises from not gaining adequate emotional closeness with people around you as a person. The thing is, this emotional loneliness starts as far back to when a child is young, one can feel like a shadow, unseen by parents who are always occupied with one thing or another. This can even occur when one becomes an adult and all of a sudden, there is no emotional connection. If such feeling of loneliness has always been present since childhood you learn the reasons why you have never been emotionally adequate.

There are many things that can aggravate a child and one of the things that can negatively affect them is to live in a household with parents who are not emotionally mature – I'm telling you this, it is a lonely experience. Therefore, if you are a parent, then you need this part, if you are a child living with immature parents, you will benefit from this part even more so. It doesn't even matter if a father or mother looks or acts like a perfect person. In fact, some parents care for their child and they take care of them when they physically hurt themselves, or look after their general health, but they never ever make any emotional connection with their kids. If a parent doesn't make a proper emotional connection with their child, they will leave an emptiness in their children's lives that needs to be filled.

The feeling of isolation creeps up on a child because they are ignored by their parents, and this can cause a lot of deep rooted hurt, sometimes, people won't notice and other times, people around will take note. You see, feeling isolated when it comes to emotions, can be an isolated experience, and may not be easily noticed by others. It will make any child, or let's say most kids, feel empty.. There are people who roll their eyes when they hear people talk about things such as feeling isolated, they think it's not even real, but the truth is, it is very real and it occurs due to a child's family.

Many children find it difficult to recognize when there's a lack of emotional understanding with their parents. It is definitely not something kids really know. However, some kids are so smart they can already spot their parent's weakness and lack of maturity even from a mile. These kids start having the sinking feeling of loneliness, which is what causes emptiness.

When a child has parents that are extremely emotionally immature, that child will try to force a connection. The child usually keeps returning to the parents and tries until, in the end, they give up. One thing about an immature parent is that they are always too afraid of a child's deep rooted feelings, they prefer not to acknowledge it.

When the kids of psychological sensitive parents are all grown up, there will be remnants of emptiness in such a child, even if they grow up to have a normal adulthood. The dangerous aspect of having emotionally immature parents is that the child keeps growing lonely until they are adults and when it's time to choose a relationship or life partner, they now realize they don't need any emotional connection because they have had to manage without it all of their lives. Such children will do normal things every other child with a happy childhood do; they work, go to school with other people, marry and raise children. But, have you ever wondered how such a child raises their own children? Well, keep reading; this chapter will look deeper into what emotional maturity is all about and its adverse effect.

Emotional Intimacy

Getting attached to people emotionally is a lot. It comprises how you get to know people and defines to whom you can tell your private things to and vent all your frustrations to about anything going on in your life.

When you have someone to vent to, you will never feel unsafe when it's time to open up. The good thing about venting to someone is that it can be in terms of words, expression of emotions or just staying quiet, but still, you know they are there for you. As the saying goes, a problem shared is a problem halved.

Being close to someone emotionally is a beautiful feeling and it is fulfilling, because you begin to see that people accept and see you for who you are. Note this though emotional closeness can only occur when the person around you decides they want to learn more about you as a person. They are not there to judge you but just to know you and be friends with you. Now, listen, a father can be a friend to his son or his daughter. You see, I have always been a believer of friendship and the thing about friendship is that friendship among family is what will bring that emotional intimacy. I will never vent my frustrations to someone I don't trust or see as a friend neither will I get close to such person. A parent needs to draw their children close to be able to get to know them. Parents who have taken it upon themselves to be close to their children emotionally will always make their kids feel welcome. Such kids do not need to bottle up feelings or troubles they are going through in school. Immature parents lack emotional strength but mature fathers and mothers always make their children have that emotional intimacy which helps their children trust them, and consequently, others too. These set of fathers and mothers have a stable emotional life and most times, these parents are steady in their concentration and attention to their children.

Emotional Loneliness

Immaturity, what do you think it is? A lot of people hate being called immature, but every human is a unique mixture and we are all ignorant of our childish side but like I said, we are a mixture of unique traits: an immature person can also be wise sometimes.

Now you must know this, parents who are not emotionally mature are always selfish and occupied by one thing or another. See, immature parents are child-like in nature too and are never comfortable with their emotional needs and so, they can't even provide any emotional support for their kids. Parents who lack emotional closeness are fidgety when it comes to being the parent and might even get angry at their kids unnecessarily and this ends up upsetting their children. Constant shouting at a child will make the child shut down emotionally. Such a child wouldn't trust anyone ever again neither will he or she reach out for any type of emotional support.

So, How do Kids Cope With Feeling Lonely?

Emotional isolation can be very frustrating and a child who has such problems will turn towards anything to make them feel better. They turn to anything just to get the attention of a parent and get the love they deserve. Some kids who go through these things usually start putting people first before satisfying themselves because that is what it takes, right? A kid who has immature parents will tend to do things, make sacrifices instead of receiving the emotional care from a parent. Nevertheless, you ask why does a child do this right? Well, kids who do this try to convince themselves that they do not have any emotional need. What's worse is that when kids over work themselves and try to act like they don't need any emotional bond with a parent, they end up being lonely. They are good at covering up whatever their needs are and thereby preventing any sincere emotional bond with anyone. It's a sad thing but children are meant to enjoy their childhood years of being a child while the adults are expected to be there for them. Loneliness is real and it's definitely something parents should look out for, you don't want a situation whereby the child acts like the adult consequently losing out on their childhood years. No child should ever experience adulthood when they are only a child. Let your children look forward to adulthood but they should live in the moment of their childhood.

Start Believing In Your Instincts

Emotionally undeveloped fathers and mothers can't recognize ways to authorize their children's emotional state and nature. Devoid of this support, kids will end up giving in to everything people advise them to do. Children may come to believe it's up to them to make the relationship with their parents work. When such child becomes an adult they may give excuses as to why they got into a terrible relationship, as if it's okay to fight everyday just to get along with their partner. Although, it's necessary to put work into a relationship for it to go smoothly, it should never feel like continuous, fruitless work.

Let me tell you now, plain and simple: it is real emotional loneliness that leads to pushing too hard for a relationship to work when your partner isn't doing anything to make it work. Teaching a child to trust and to know he or she is loved will make a child trust in his or herself to know when emotional satisfaction comes.

Emotional solitude originates from having little or no emotional bond. It can begin during the childhood of a person, by feeling like a shadow and not being seen by parents who are always occupied. Let's say it's been a lifetime feeling, and it shows that there are no sustainable emotions for the individual as a child.

Emotional Solitude Knows No Gender

Research has shown that still more women reach out for therapy then men. Nevertheless, I've seen a lot of men too who have problems of loneliness in their relationships. What's even more difficult for men is that, society has done more harm than good. Society tends to highlight the emotional needs and problems of women more than those of men and this leads to men becoming cagey and making them less open about sharing their emotions and relationship problems. However, when we check out the rate at which people commit suicide everyday, we can see men have emotions too. Many men are likely to turn out to be violent or end up committing suicide when they are going through terrible emotional problems. It's important to note that any man that does not have the ability to be emotionally intimate and seek care from people they think should care about them, end up feeling empty. Know this though, a man will always resist from showing his feelings. Emotional bonds are very basic human needs regardless of the gender of a person.

Chapter 2

Understanding who is an Emotionally Immature Parent

Most of the signals of underdevelopment in emotions are beyond the control of people who are immature. It's so bad that most parents who are very immature don't recognize it. What's even worse is that it always has an adverse effect on their kids. The point of this chapter is not to heap blames on immature parents but to make you as a reader understand why there are such parents.

Luckily, as grown-ups, we acquire the capability and freedom to evaluate whether our fathers and mothers will be able to give us the attention and kindness we yearn for. In order to actually review this accurately, it's significant to realize not only your fathers' and mothers' shallow traits, but also their core emotional background. The moment you really get these behavioural patterns of your parents, that is when you begin to value or study things to expect from your father or mother, so then you can list down their traits and you will not be trapped by their limits. Make sure you have one thing in mind though, that your fathers or mothers are private people. Right now, they don't know you've been doing your research as to why they are so aloof, but that's the point, they don't need to know. As you read though, also note that this book is especially useful for both parties: parents and children. The aim of this book is so that you can expand the self-assurance that emanates from your story. Don't feel bad if you are child and you've ordered this book; you've done nothing wrong and it doesn't mean you are trying to see your parents in bad light. But it will teach you to know them more and learn a thing or two about yourself as a person.

Just like you've seen in the introduction and first chapter, emotionally undeveloped parents may cause an adverse effect on their children's emotional growth and the relationships they will have when they become adults. These adverse effects usually stem from minor to severe, but it all depends on the parent's level of emotional immaturity, and also the effect is similar on children that feel lonely.

Behavioural Pattern Vs. Temporary Emotional Relapse

As you read this chapter, you will learn the difference between a behavioural patterns and something that is just a temporary emotional problem. Any person can momentarily lose emotional guidance or be abrupt when exhausted or stressed. A lot of us have so much to feel ashamed of when we think of some things we did back in time. However, if someone has behavioural patterns of emotional underdevelopment, such an attitude will likely shows up constantly. These personalities are so involuntary that most people don't even know they are doing them. Emotionally underdeveloped people will never think back to their behaviour and see what it does to people around them. Unlike normal people who think back and feel embarrassed about their attitude, they don't feel anything at all. They regret nothing.

Behavioural Patterns Connected With Emotional Underdevelopment

Emotionally Undeveloped people have a list of traits which you are going to learn as you read this chapter. Their personalities are interconnected and they display various patterns and reactions to things. In the chapters that follow after this, you'll keep getting more things about parents with emotional immaturity and how to handle them.

Emotionally Undeveloped People Are Very Stiff And Selfish

You must know that when people with an immature mind have a way around something, they'll go for it and even go as far as getting that goal without caring about people they stamp on in the way. Although, when they are in a relationship or make decisions that involve emotions, they become useless. It's not their fault but they are so stiff or impetuous, and most times when they manage with things in life, they take the easy way around things.

Emotionally Immature People Can't Handle Stress

Another thing you should note about immature people is that they hate stress. It's not something they can deal with so they freak out when they are under pressure. Now, imagine a parent who can't handle stress. How do you think they will be parents? Immature people will never accept their wrong-doings they would rather push the blame on to people around them. It's easier for them to do that and you know why? The moment an emotionally immature person is under pressure, they get upset and it becomes a lot of hard work for them to handle things and they are always in need to be pampered every single time even when they are wrong.

Immature People Only Do What Soothes Them

Have you ever noticed how children throw tantrums? Okay, let me explain it this way: young children are always happy when they get what they want and unhappy – which leads to tantrums – when they don't get what they want. Did you notice I used two key emotions most humans feel? Happy and unhappy! Yes, children function based on their emotions alone. But you realize as we grow things change for us and we start to take charge of what we feel and even if we can't control how we feel, we do not let that control us. But that's not the same with emotionally immature people. Immature people act out on what they are feeling, they never keep calm to handle things logically. Mature people think first then act but it is never the same for immature people.

They Don't Know How To Respect Other People's Point Of View

People who have difficulty with their emotions are so

immature that they get angry when people have their own ideas. They are terrible with arguments because they always end up fighting with the other party. They want people to see things their way and never have their own opinion. They get so comfortable in situations that they believe everyone must have the same beliefs and such beliefs must correlate with theirs.

Emotionally Immature People Are Always Conceited

Regular kids are self-centred when they are very young, but this should disappear by the time they become adults, if it doesn't then they end up being arrogant or emotionally immature adults. However, children are absolutely different from adults who are conceited though. When adults are conceited, joy and honesty is always absent from them.

When someone is immature, they are likely to be selfish because they always make excuses for their failures by stating they are occupied with something. In fact, emotionally undeveloped people are fixated on something in a crazy way that is totally different from a child's way of obsession. Kids are deep-rooted in this unending state of uncertainty, being afraid that maybe soon their peers will see them as bad, insufficient, or unlovable. But pause though before you begin to feel bad for your kids, you must know that their defences work flawlessly to subdue their nervousness below so that an adult won't even notice.

People Who Are Emotionally Immature Always Reference Themselves

People who are not emotionally mature tend to have discussions that will always lead back to them. Do you get it? They never want to have discussions where they will not get the chance to tell the other person "Like me." When emotionally immature people want to have a discussion they want the focus to be on them. They are less concerned about what new things they might learn in a discussion they just want it to centre on them alone.

People who are not emotionally mature are not good with social skills so even when they have a discussion, they are never polite and they do not listen. Note that it doesn't mean these people openly change the discussion, but they are never interested in your discussion. They won't even ask questions about your experience on the said topic in fact, they might keep quiet or ask questions about something entirely different just to diffuse the discussion.

Now, do you wonder if there are a lot of emotionally undeveloped parents?

I'll tell you this now: Yes, there are many parents who are not so mature with their emotions and I know you must wonder how the hell they will raise kids. But before we keep making up questions, how about you ask yourself this: what led these emotionally immature parents to turn out like this? It's mostly because they shut down emotionally as kids. Their parents weren't there for them emotionally either and the cycle continues, it becomes a loop

People Who Are Immature Emotionally Can Be Unpredictable And Conflicting

Many people who are emotionally immature don't have a well formed personality. They have different parts of them that make up their personalities. I know you think that is the way humans should be right? You think we should be complex and I totally agree but it's not normal to have a contradictory personality. Humans are not some kind of vehicle where parts can be bought so it can work, so, it's weird to have clumps of contradictory personality.

Although, I understand that this happens due to the fact that they never conveyed their emotions as a child. So, they become adults that are often emotionally conflicting. Their traits are feebly organized, and end up showing emotions that conflict. They are always in and out of their emotions and they won't notice how inconsistent their emotions have become.

Emotionally immature people judge things through the physical and avoid using emotions

Parents who are emotionally undeveloped usually do a good job providing for everything physical their children might need. They buy clothes, pay their bills, provide food etc. for their kids but they will never go further than that. When it comes to physical needs they make sure they provide everything that will help their children. These needs will be granted to their kids so far as it is something they can provide with their money and in their own capacity. That provision stops once it becomes an emotional need and they just switch off without any explanation.

Some children will be taken care of when they fall ill and get their parent's attention but this only happens when their parents are certain they are really sick. They were able to experience this care alone only after they were confirmed to be truly sick. It will likely be the only time such a child will receive any form of emotional connection with their parent.

Such immature people get confused with emotions. They don't even know what to do when it has to do with things that involve emotions, you can't blame them though, and they were likely never brought up by parents who gave them love or showed emotions. Such people follow the footsteps of their parents and so they only remember their parents ever being there for them physically. Although they also feel this pang of hurt for not been taken care of emotionally, they won't provide that to their kids because they don't know what it feels like to have an emotional bond with someone and they don't know how to achieve it

Emotionally immature people can be sadists

They dread genuine emotions especially ones that expresses happiness so in order to stop feeling this dread, emotionally immature people resort into ruining the moment. So when such people become parents, they will change the subject or warn their kids not to get their hopes up when their children are excited. Just to bring down their children's happiness and say something that shows unconcern.

People Who Are Immature Emotionally Are Also Shallow With Their Thinking

People who are not mature with their emotions can become overcome by emotions very easily, and they show their nervousness by transforming such emotions. So rather than have deep feelings, they handle things and act sketchily. The way they react to things only shows one thing which is that they're zealous and very passionate, but the way they express their emotions mostly have oblique values.

Chapter 3

What do the affected children go through

The way emotionally immature parents handle their relationships with their children can be quite frustrating and often always affects the emotional needs of their children. Growing up with such parents can be very lonely, draining and exasperating.

During our childhood, the strongest bond and primary attachment we have is that which we feel for our parents. When hungry, scared, tired, or ill, they are the first people we turn to.

The absence of this bond helps explain why relationships with emotionally immature parents are so disappointing. Our instincts prompt us to keep turning to our parents for care and understanding. The following are some of the difficulties of having an emotionally immature parent.

1. It Is Difficult To Communicate With Them

An emotionally immature parent has poor communication skills. Interacting with them is very frustrating; they make others feel like they have been shut down, or shut out. They have a very limited range of attention when it comes to the interests of other people.

Interacting with emotionally immature people is usually one-sided. They are not interested in having reciprocal conversations; they hunger for exclusive attention and want everyone to show interest in what they are interested in. If they are no longer the center of attention, they find ways to bring back the attention to them.

2. They Stimulate Anger In Their Children

Anger is an adaptive reaction to feelings of neglect, rejection and abandonment. It is a sign of distress to unhealthy emotional situations. Feelings of anger or rage are perfectly normal reactions to emotional injury.

In some cases, the children of emotionally immature parents will either suppress their anger or turn it on themselves. When anger is internalized like this, people will criticize and find faults with themselves. They can end up extremely depressed or even have suicidal thoughts; thoughts of suicide can be said to be the ultimate manifestation of anger in opposition to the self. Other people manifest their anger is in a passive-aggressive way; manifesting behaviors like forgetting, lying, or avoiding. In this way, they are trying to get the better of their parents or person in authority.

3. They Interact With Their Children By Emotional Contagion

Emotionally immature people have very little emotional experiences, and instead of talking about their emotional needs, they usually act them out. The method of communication they use is known as emotional contagion (Hatfield, Rapson, and Le 2007). This communication method attempts to get other people to feel what they are feeling.

Emotional contagion is how babies and little children communicate. They cry until the people around them understand what is wrong and take steps to fix it. Emotional contagion from a distressed baby motivates a caretaker to do all they can to comfort the child.

Emotionally immature adults convey their feelings in this way. When they are distressed or upset everyone around them scrambles to do all they can to make them feel better. In this way, the child catches the distress of the parent and feels obligated to make the parent feel better. However, if the parent is not willing to understand his/her own feelings, nothing will ever get resolved. Instead, their upset feelings spread to everyone else, so that everyone responds without truly understanding what the matter is.

4. They Avoid Doing Emotional Work

Emotionally immature parents never try to understand the emotions of other people. If they are accused of being insensitive, they dismiss the situation by claiming that the hurt person is overly sensitive. They attempt to rationalize their hasty and thoughtless responses. The way they respond shows that they cannot be bothered to take the effort to understand the emotions of other people, or are unable to

5. It Is Hard To Give To Them

Emotionally immature people want other people to pay attention to their needs, but it is very difficult to give to them. Researcher Leigh McCoullough (McCoullough et Al. 2003), calls this poor receptive capacity. They want others to show interest in their problems, but it is very unlikely that they respond to helpful suggestions. They instinctively reject efforts to make them feel cared for. They drag other people in, but when they try to help, they chase them away.

In addition to this, they expect other people to read their minds and get angry if people do not quickly anticipate their wishes (McCullough et al. 2003). Instead of telling people what they need, they hold back, waiting to see if anyone will notice how they feel. They create a toxic guessing game that leaves everybody uneasy.

6. They Avoid Working To Repair Their Relationships

Problems will definitely arise in a relationship. When they do crop up, it is important to work on addressing and solving the conflict. The ability of admitting to being wrong and working on making things better requires maturity. Emotionally immature people do not like to own up to their mistakes; they expect people to let them off the hook immediately. In fact, it is possible for them to blame others if they are not forgiven immediately.

After a falling out, people try to repair the relationship

by apologizing, seeking forgiveness, or making amends. John Gottman calls this a repair attempt. Unfortunately, emotionally immature people are completely oblivious to what forgiveness means. Forgiveness to them means to make it as if the rift never occurred. They are completely unaware that people require emotional processing or time to rebuild trust after a falling out. The only thing they want is for things to go back to the way they were. The pain of others is unimportant.

7. They Expect Their Children To Mirror Them

Emotionally responsive parents are able to mirror the feelings of their children by showing the same emotions on their faces (Winnicott 1971). They display concern when their children are distressed, and show enthusiasm when their children are elated. In this manner, they teach their children about emotions and show them how to spontaneously engage others. This also gives their children the feeling of being seen and understood as a unique individual.

However, emotionally immature parents, expect their children to understand and mirror them. They get extremely upset if their children do not act the way that they want them to. It is unfortunate that it is not psychologically possible for a child to accurately mirror an adult.

Emotionally immature parents delude themselves into thinking that their kids will make them feel good about themselves. When their children start to develop their own needs, it can drive them to a state of intense anxiety. In some cases, they use threats of punishment, and abandonment as an attempt to gain control and reinforce their self-esteem—at the expense of their children.

8. Their Self-Esteem Is Dependent On Their Children's Compliance

For emotionally immature people, they are only able to feel good about themselves when they are able to manipulate other people into giving them what they want and acting the way they think they should. With their shaky self-worth, they find it difficult to tolerate the emotions of their children. If their child is upset, they start to question whether they are good or bad. If they are unable to calm the child, they may feel like a failure, and reproach the child for making them feel that way.

In fact, their interactions with other people boils down to whether they are the good people or the bad ones. This clarifies their intense defensiveness if you attempt talking to them about something they did. They prefer to shut down communication, rather than listen to something that makes them feel like they are the bad people.

9. Roles Are Sacred And Important To Them

Role compliance is extremely important to emotionally immature parents. Roles help to make life easy and allow decisions to be made more conveniently. They require their children to play a proper role, and that includes respect and obedience to them. They employ the use of clichés to crop the dominance of their role as a parent because they reduce the complexity of situations and generally make life easier. As a result of how important roles are to them, they exhibit the following:

- They feel a sense of entitlement because of their social role

This is a point of view that expects certain treatment because of a social role. Emotionally immature parents behave as though being a parent means they can stop respecting other peoples boundaries or being considerate. When people feel entitled to act as they wish, this can be said to be role entitlement.

- They coerce other people to act out certain roles

They can also coerce other people to act out a role because they want them to. They force their children to act a certain way by not giving them the silent treatment, threatening to reject them, or getting other members of the family to attack them. When their children do things that they do not approve, they make them feel guilty.

Emotionally immature parents are not comfortable with complex situations and prefer life simplified, thus they have no hesitations about creating role for others. To them, if a person is not fulfilling a supposed role, it means that something is wrong with them and they need to change.

10. They Seek Enmeshment, Not Emotional Intimacy

Emotional intimacy and enmeshment are two ways of interaction that look similar, but are actually very different. Emotional intimacy involves two individuals with a confident sense of self getting to deeply understands and know each other on every level, as well as building emotional trust. This intimacy is refreshing and stimulates the personal growth of an individual, as a result of the interest and support that they enjoy from another person.

Contrarily, enmeshment allows for two emotionally immature people to find their identity in an highly dependent relationship (Bowen 1978). Each person plays a convenient role for the other, and by relying on this, they are able to develop a sense of security in the relationship. In cases where a person tries to detach himself/herself from the role, the other feels an apprehension that can only be eased by a return to the assigned role.

Their desire for enmeshment gives rise to the following.

- They play favorites

Playing favorites is a manifestation of enmeshment (Libby 2010). Their favoritism is probably because the psychological level of the preferred child's maturity is similar to that of the parent (Bowen 1978). People with a low level of emotional maturity tend to draw others into mutual enmeshment. This is especially so if they are parent and child.

Enmeshment can be either a dependency or an idealization. Dependent enmeshment allows the parent to play the role of either the rescuer or the victim when the child is distressed. Idealized enmeshment allows the parent to dote on a favorite child as though the child is of higher importance and more deserving.

Emotionally immature parents are so needy for enmeshment that they are capable of acting it out with people that are not part of their family. If they are unable to satisfy their need for an enmeshment, they can go outside their family in search of it.

11. They Have A Poor Sense Of Time

This point is extremely subtle and easily overlooked. Emotionally immature people have a fractured orientation to time; this is especially so when they get emotional. This is a reason why the lives of emotionally immature people are often plagued with problems; they do not see them coming. They are ruled by desires of the moment, frequently disconnected with their experiences in time. When they act, they do not use the past for guidance, and they do not expect the future. This results in their inconsistences and the unreflective way they manage issues in their relationships.

When emotionally stressed or aroused, they do not experience themselves as being a part of the ongoing flow of time. Their experiences of different moments in time are like unrelated, nonlinear glitches that go on and off randomly, with little or no linkages between one interaction and another. The moments of their lives feel disconnected, each affecting the others, and all affecting their relationships with other because their consciousness jumps from one experience to another, they act inconsistently. This is a reason why they become annoyed when you point out their past behavior. They see the past as the past; the past is gone and is of no significance to the present. In the same vein, they are likely to dismiss your caution about something in the future; the future is yet to arrive

- Their poor sense of time can be confused with emotional manipulation

It may look like emotionally immature people are emotional manipulators, but in actual fact they are just very shrewd tactician, that press for whatever feels best at the time. They have no interest in being consistent; therefore, they say whatever grants them the upper hand in the moment, especially in tense moments. In their work or other pursuits, they may be capable of thinking strategically, but in emotional situations, they prefer to go for the immediate advantage. An example of this is lying; it gives a fleeting win that feels good in the moment, but in the long run, it is detrimental to a relationship.

- Their poor sense of time restricts their self-reflection and accountability

The ability to review your thoughts and behaviors over time is self-reflection. Those that focus mostly on the present do not have enough of a perspective on time to devote themselves to self-reflection. With each experience, they leave their past behind, freeing them from any sense of responsibility they might have for their actions. They are unable to understand why other people cannot forgive, forget, and move on; their limited sense of time, makes them unable to understand that it takes time to heal from a conflict.

Accountability would be very hard for them. For those that do not feel a temporal connection between their actions and the consequences it may have in the future, accountability is a flimsy concept. This behavior is a result of their lack of self-development, their badly integrated personality, and their inclination towards extremely rigid, literal thinking.

In summary

Emotionally immature people lack a firm sense of their personal history, and resist accountability for their actions in the past or the consequences it may have in the future. They see family closeness and emotional intimacy as enmeshment. Real communication is almost impossible with them because of their poor empathy and their insistence on roles. They neglect repairing their relationships, and avoid the emotional work need to be thoughtful of other people, instead focusing on whether other people make them look good or bad.

Chapter 4

Different ways of being an Emotionally Immature Parent

There are different types of emotionally immature parents; irrespective of these different types, they all cause insecurity and loneliness in their children's lives.

Despite the differences in the emotionally immature parent, they all exhibit certain characteristics common to emotionally immature people; they are self-involved, narcissistic, emotionally unreliable, egocentric, insensitive, and have a limited capacity for expressing genuine emotional intimacy. They all narrow down and distort reality rather than deal with it; they make their children the adult; are unable to resonate with the feelings of other people, and have poor stress tolerance.

In addition to this, all four types are unable to see their children as unique individuals and instead interact with them strictly in accordance with their own needs. With all four types of emotionally immature parents, their children end up losing their sense of self because their needs and interests are overshadowed by what is important to their parents.

The Four Types of Emotionally Immature Parents

Even though each type sabotages the emotional security of a child in different ways, they all relate with their children with very little empathy, their emotional support is unreliable, and their basic lack of sensitivity is the same. They all exist along a spectrum, from mild to severe, and the degree of narcissism varies along each type. In some severe cases, the parent may be mentally ill, and even physically or sexually abusive. The following are the types of emotionally immature parents.

1. The Emotional Parent
2. The Driven Parent
3. The Rejecting Parent
4. The Passive Parent

Most emotionally immature parents tend to fall into one category, but there may be cases where they exhibit behaviors that fall under a different type.

The Emotional Parent

Emotional parents are ruled by their feelings. One minute, they could be actively involved in something, and the next, they withdraw abruptly. They are unstable, unpredictable and overwhelmed by anxiety.

Emotional parents are the most childlike of all four types. Around them, you are walking on eggshells; they give the notion that they need to be carefully watched over and handled. They get upset easily, and once they are, the entire family rushes to soothe them. When the emotional parent has a breakdown, they drag their children into their personal meltdown. Their children most often experience the intensity of their despair, fury, or hatred. The most predictable thing about them is their volatile and unstable emotions.

There are two types of the emotional parent. The first type are those who from a psychological point of view, are actually mentally ill. They may be bipolar, psychotic, or exhibit traits of narcissistic or borderline personality disorder. Their unrestrained emotionality can result in physical attacks on other people or even attempts at suicide. People feel uneasy around them because there is no telling when their emotions will escalate. They also have suicidal tendencies. The looming threat of suicide will be so terrifying to their children, who will bear the weight of doing all they can to keep their parent alive.

The second, milder type are those that are emotionally unstable. Their emotional unreliability is a big issue, and forms the basis of cyclothymic disorder or histrionic personality disorder, which is often marked by fluctuating occurrences of high and low moods.

All emotional parents struggle with tolerating stress and emotional stimulation, irrespective of how severe it is. They are unable to adequately maintain a balance on their emotions and behaviors in situations that mature adults should be able to handle. Because of this they are prone to substance abuse, which makes them even more unhinged and inadequate to tolerate frustration or discomfort.

The emotional parents sees the world only in black-and-white, keeps score, holds grudges, and is adept at controlling and manipulating others with emotional tactics. Their alternating moods and reactions make them unreliable and intimidating. They act helpless and see themselves as victims, and as a result, their family life revolves around them and their moods. Outside the family, where there is a structured role to follow, they are able to control their emotions, but within the boundaries of an intimate family relationship, the full extent of their unstableness and impulsivity is displayed.

The children of emotional parents develop a sense of subjugating themselves to the wishes of other people (Young and Klosko 1993). Because they grew up preparing for when next their parents lose control of their emotions, they tend to be excessively attentive to the feelings and moods of other people, often ignoring theirs in the process. This is very detrimental to the state of their mental health.

The Driven Parent

Driven parents are perfectionists, goal-oriented and always busy. They are controlling, often interfering in the lives of their children, but never really taking the time to develop true empathy for their children.

Driven parents appear to be the most normal of all four

types of emotionally immature people. They may even seem to be remarkably invested in their children's lives. They are driven people, thus they are consistently obsessed with getting things done. Emotional parents are oblivious to their immaturity, but driven parents seem to be so dedicated to their child's success that it is difficult to see and notice how egocentric they are. It is quite difficult to spot anything unhealthy about them, however, their children struggle with either taking initiative or self-control.

Interestingly, the children of these involved, hardworking parents are often unmotivated, and even depressed.

A closer examination will allow you to detect the emotional immaturity present in these reputable, competent people. Their emotional immaturity is seen in how they make assumptions about other people, presuming that they will want and value the same things that they do. Their excessive perfectionist and self-centered behavior, births a conviction that they know what is best for others.

They do not self-reflect and thus, they do not experience self-doubt, or see how their behavior impacts others. They would rather pretend that everything has worked out and that they have all the answers.

They are unable to accept any contrary interests that their children may have, rather pushing for what they want to see. In addition to their lack of empathy, the motivation to achieve their goals comes before the feelings of other people, including their children.

Driven parents are often self-made. They grew up quickly in an emotionally deprived environment. They learnt to be independent early on and get by on their own efforts rather than on the nurturing of their parents. Driven parents fear that their children will not succeed; hence, they are unable to offer their children the unconditional acceptance that would give them the courage and determination from which they go out and achieve their goals.

Consciously or unconsciously, they put their children under constant evaluation. This constant evaluation prevents their children from seeking adult help for anything. This results in their children resisting potential mentors and teachers while growing up.

Because the driven parent is certain that he knows best, he is prone to doing eccentric things. For instance, they can drop by unannounced and start rearranging the apartment of their adult children like its theirs. They end up feeling hurt when they are told to stop doing outlandish things like that.

They are emotionally insensitive and completely out of sync with their children's experiences. They cannot adapt to the needs of their children. They compel their children to do what they believe he/she should do, and as a result, their children always feel like they should be doing more, or something different from what they are currently doing.

The Passive Parent

Passive parents have an attitude of leaving things to develop on their own and avoid dealing or interfering with anything that seems upsetting. They seem less harmful than the other types of emotionally immature people, but the effects they have on their children are often more devastating.

They bend over backwards to a dominant partner, and look the other way when abuse and neglect occurs. They get by, by minimizing actual problems and acquiescing.

Their behavior makes you question why they even have a family. Whether their behavior is mild or appalling, they do not enjoy emotional intimacy and make it clear that they do not want to be bothered by their children.

Unlike the other types of emotionally immature people, passive parents are not angry or pushy. They are however intolerant of other people's needs, acquiesce to people with more dominant personalities and they communicate with others by issuing commands, often flaring up, or separating themselves from their family life. In cases where they take part in family activities, they still show little or no closeness or engagement with other members of the family. They prefer to be left alone to do their own thing.

They may seem to be more emotionally available than the other types of emotionally immature people, but their emotional availability is only up to a certain point. They become passive, emotionally withdrawn, and hide themselves when things become intense. They fail to offer their children guidance or provide limits that will help them navigate their life and the world around them. In simple terms, they may love you, but they are unable to help you.

Passive parents are just as immature and self-involved as the other types. They seem more lovable and accepting than the other three types due to their easy-going and generally playful personalities. In fact, they can show empathy for their children, as long as it does not get in the way of their needs. Because they are also egocentric, it is more probable for passive parents to use their children to meet their emotional needs- the primary need to be the focus of someone else's doting attention. They enjoy the innocence of their child and are often the favorite parent; the child spends most of his/her time with this parent. However, because the child is filling the parent's need for an attentive, admiring companion, it becomes a form of emotional incest. The child is never completely comfortable in the relationship because it runs the risk of making the other parent envious; the relationship may even feel sexualized.

While they often enjoy their children, spend time to have fun with them and make them feel special, the children can sense that their parents are not really there for them in any significant way. Their kids are aware of the fact that it is best not to expect or ask for much from this parent. In actuality, these parents are notorious for ignoring family situations that are detrimental to their children's wellbeing. They frequently leave their kids to look after themselves. In challenging times, there have been cases where these parents leave the family for the chance at a happier life. Even if the parent is the passive type, because they are more emotionally available, the pain felt by the child can cut very deep; this is because the abandonment arose from the parent that meant the most to the child.

When growing up, the passive parent learnt to steer clear of the line of fire, they had a low profile, kept themselves unseen and allowed people with stronger personalities to walk all over them. This is why as adults; they are oblivious to the fact that it is their job to not only have a good time with their children, but to also protect them. In moments where they are really needed, they go into a kind of trance, turtling into themselves or finding some other complacent means to lay low.

Children that idolize their passive parents are liable to become adults that make excuses for the inexcusable behavior of other people. This is because they were ignorant of the fact that it was their parents' duty to look after their emotional interests. They saw them as helpless and victims of their circumstances. They are often caught off guard by the idea that their amazing, lovely parent actually had an obligation to look out for them when they were unable to protect themselves as children. They have never considered that it is the responsibility of parents to put the emotional welfare of their children at the very least on an equal footing with their own interests.

The Rejecting Parent

The rejecting parent seems to have a constant wall around them. Spending time with their children seems like a waste to them and they would much rather prefer it if they were left alone to their devices. Such parents are withdrawn, dismissive and demeaning.

They give their children the feeling that they would be okay if they did not have to look after them. Their irritated demeanor stops their children from approaching them. They reject any attempt to draw them into affectionate or emotional interactions. They may become angry or abusive if they are pressured into responding emotionally. They may even come to view his/her child as a burden, that is getting in the way of him/her pursuing his/her own life goals. In this manner, the child is both loathed and essentially rejected.

In the family, everything revolves around their wishes. They could be like the scary, cold and aloof father that rules the family with an iron fist. His needs must be immediately seen to, everyone walks on thin ice around him; the family does all they can to avoid upsetting him.

The rejecting parent is also the most inferior of all four types when it comes to being empathetic. They use evasive mechanisms such as avoiding eye contact, using a blank look or an unfriendly stare to signal their disdain for emotional intimacy and make others go away.

The children of rejecting parents grow up seeing themselves as a bother and a source of irritation. This encourages them to give up easily. As adults, they find it difficult to ask for what they want, even when it is freely available.

In summary

While there may be four different types of emotionally immature parents, they are all self-involved, insensitive and emotionally unavailable. They are difficult to communicate and connect with due to their lack of empathy. Their fear of genuine emotion makes them seek to be controlling in a bid to comfort them, thus their children feel emotionally unseen. They are all exhausting to be around, and they have a need to always be the center of attention. They are incapable of genuine companionship with other people.

Chapter 5

Behavioural patterns of Children with Emotionally Immature Parents

Failure of immature parents to emotionally interact with their children and provide them with the needed fondness and attention leads to the children developing coping mechanisms to make up for the lack of attention. The children conjure healing fantasies that their attention deficiency will somehow be rectified. In addition, children cope by creating a role-self thus conjuring a special family role for themselves, the whole point of the role-self is to get attention from the "uncaring" parents.

To cope with emotional neglect, children often use these two different coping mechanisms which are: internalizing or externalizing. Of these two coping mechanisms, neither makes a child reach his full potential. Due to being neglected by the parents, a child starts to re-evaluate his self-worth and feels like he is not enough to gain his parent's attention. This then causes him to start behaving to be someone who he is not. This then suppresses the child's natural identity which includes his innate aptitudes and genuine feelings as he begins to act in a way that he believes will draw his parent's attention to him.

Healing Fantasies: The Root

A healing fantasy is a story we tell ourselves to help us believe that we'll be happier in the future. This happens to every kid with emotionally immature parents as these children have to deal with their parent's emotional limitations while they themselves are being emotionally deprived and so they come up with this story, this fantasy, a healing fantasy.

Children often change themselves and other people to fit a certain role, to be someone different from who they really are because they think that the cure for their childhood loneliness lies in doing that and this is the theme of all healing fantasies. Healing fantasies most often begin with "*If only.*" and an example is when people think that they will get more attention if only they are important enough, rich enough or attractive enough. The healing fantasy is merely a solution that stems from a child's mind and it doesn't actually fit in adult realities. The healing fantasy, however, gives the child hope to get through a painful and miserable childhood.

Healing Fantasies: How They Affect Adult Relationships

As adults, children who survived childhood by creating healing fantasies will secretly expect their closet relationships to fulfill their healing fantasies and they build up expectations for their friends and other people with the fantasies as the basis. The expectations built up from these fantasies are often times self-defeating.

Sometimes, there is a little realization that they're

trying to force their healing fantasy on someone but it can actually be observed in 'little tests of love" that people go through. An outsider will easily see that the fantasy is unrealistic. Marriage therapies often help people to see how they're forcing their fantasy on their partner.

Developing a Role-Self

Developing a role-self is not something you set out to do deliberately, the process is unconscious. It is the creation of a pseudo-self that will give a secure place in the family system. After some time, the role self gradually replaces the true self. Developing a role-self is a way of trying to create a connection when parents or caregivers do not respond adequately to the true self. The role-self is created through trial and error and viewing other people's reactions.

When children who have developed role-selves become adults, they keep playing this role desperately and secretly wishing that someone would give them attention just as they wished their parents had. Role-selves can have positive or negative characters; this is because not every child possesses the internal resources to achieve success or has self-control in their interaction with others. Genetics and neurology also play a role in some children as it pushes them into impulsive reactivity and not constructive action.

Sometimes, emotionally immature parents do subconsciously use different children in the family to show parts of their own role-self and healing fantasies, and this can be a reason for a negative role-self in their children. An example is tagging a child as the perfect one and dubbing the other as the black sheep of the family.

Developing a Role-Self: The Influence of Parents

It is rare for parents to consciously try to undermine their child's future but they allow their own anxiety to cloud their senses and make them see only the negative and undesirable activities in their children, this is actually beyond their control as it is a very powerful physiological defense mechanism.

If a child finds a role that fits his parent's needs perfectly, he will most likely identify with this role-self. During this process, however, his true self will get suppressed and will become more invisible as the child fully transforms into the role he needs to act to belong. This will have an adverse effect during adulthood as an intimate relationship can't be formed from the position of a role-self.

A problem with the role-self is that it siphons energy off of the true self as it doesn't have its own source of energy. It withdraws vitality from the true self because playing a role is way more tiring than being the true self. The role self is made up and this can breed some sort of insecurity due to fear of being exposed as a fake. Acting a role-self doesn't work in the long run because he true-self can never truly be completely suppressed.

Coping Styles with Emotionally Immature Parents

Children can react to emotionally immature parents in either of two ways: by externalizing their problems or internalizing them. In rare cases, a child can internalize and externalize. The style adopted is a function of personality rather than choice.

Internalizers:

They are mentally proactive and desire to learn. Internalizers are sensitive and they try to understand cause and effect, they see life as an opportunity for learning and self-development. On the whole, they enjoy becoming more competent. Internalizers try to solve problems by themselves and they believe that they can make things better just by working harder. The internalizer is overly self-sacrificing but later becomes resentful of how much he sacrifices for others.

Externalizers:

Externalizers are reactive, they act before they think things through. They blame other people and circumstances for their own actions. They live life without a plan but they rarely learn from their mistakes and they often require other people to step in to fix the damage caused by their impulsive actions. Externalizers have low self-confidence or a sense of superiority. Their main source of anxiety is to be cut off from the external sources of their security.

Understanding the Externalizer's Worldview

Externalizers engage in behaviors that are self-destructive and they tend to push people away while internalizers suffer in silence and blame themselves for anything that goes wrong. Externalizing keeps people from growing psychologically but internalizing promotes psychological development through self-reflection.

Externalizers Create a Cycle of Self-Defeat

Externalizing elicits punishment and rejection, they act out their depression, anxiety, and pain. They try to distract themselves from important problems by taking impulsive actions and when they face the consequences of their actions, they feel shame and failure but only for a short time as they use denial to avoid this. Externalizers blame everyone else for their actions and end up pushing everybody away and then end up not getting the emotional support they needed in the first place.

Externalizers Look for Solutions Outside Themselves

Externalizers try to dispel stress immediately when it hits and so they do not really give themselves the opportunity to grow and learn from the mistakes they make. They depend on other people to make them feel better and even carry some resentment because they feel that they should have been helped sooner. Because most externalizers do not self-reflect but look outside themselves to feel better, they don't work to have better self-control. An externalizer will most likely become an emotionally immature person if left unchecked, it can thus be inferred that most emotionally immature parents are externalizers. Mature people will deal with their problems and adapt to reality while externalizers believe that reality is shaped by their wishes.

Emotional dependency is promoted in children who are externalizers, children who externalized are often indulged by emotionally immature parents because it takes their mind away from their own unresolved problems. These parents can adopt a role-self of the strong parent helping the dependent child.

Externalizers Exist Along a Continuum of Severity

Externalizing exists in stages which can be ranked according to severity. At the top of the scale are predators and sociopaths who see others merely as resources to exploit. Milder externalizers resemble internalizers because they are nonconfrontational but they still hold the belief that others are the cause of their problems.

Externalizers can be Abusive Siblings

Externalizers can be predatory, and they tend to make life miserable for an internalizing sibling. Often times, the parents do not interfere and they see the externalizing child as special and then allow him to get away with bad behavior. Externalizing children tend to emotionally abuse their family with their troubles and tantrums and emotionally immature parents will often rescue and placate these externalizing children while telling the internalizing child to try to get along with his sibling or understand him.

The Continuum of Coping: Mixed Styles

Personality characteristics like coping styles do not exist in pure forms but instead exist along a continuum. Severe examples of internalizing and externalizing differ greatly from one another but they still occur along a spectrum. In the right situations, externalizers can exhibit attitudes and behaviors associated with internalizers and internalizers can also exhibit attitudes and behaviors associated with externalizers. When externalizers hit rock bottom when they have nothing to hold on to anymore, they can open up to the idea that they might need to change instead of expecting the world to conform to their wishes, and when internalizers are severely stressed, they can react impulsively like any externalizer.

Externalizers can be more Internalizing

Externalizing and internalizing is simply a part of being human, everyone can exhibit different severities of either style depending on circumstances and based on where they belong on the continuum. People who are open about their problems enough to seek therapy and also enjoy reading some self-help books are most likely to be internalizers.

Conversely, externalizers are far more likely to end up in treatment because of external pressures. A great part of addiction recovery is dedicated to nudging externalizers towards becoming more internalizing and thus take responsibility for their actions.

Internalizers Can Act Like Externalizers When Under Stress

When very stressed or lonely, internalizers can start to exhibit attitudes and behaviors associated with externalizers. Occasionally, self-sacrificing internalizers can start acting out their distress by having affairs or superficial sexual relations. They feel a lot of shame and guilt about this and are very much afraid of being found out, But they are still attached to these actions, these affairs as a means of escape from an emotionally barren life. Engaging in an affair helps them to feel alive and special and it also offers the possibility of their needs for attention being met outside of their primary relationship. Internalizers first try by speaking to their partners about their unhappiness but if their partner does not listen or instead rejects these overtures, then internalizers may go out looking for someone else to save them which is a characteristic behavior of an externalizer.

This can actually explain some midlife crises, where previously responsible people seem to throw away their values in very surprising ways. They begin seeking a more personally rewarding life and can start rejecting obligations and responsibilities. Examining the internalizer's profile, it can be said that the midlife crisis is not so sudden but it is as a result of years of self-denial followed by a realization that they put other people's needs before theirs too many times. Furthermore, internalizers can resort to substance abuse as a way to deal with stress.

The Importance of Balance

People who are at the extremes of the externalizer or internalizer continuum usually experience many problems in life. Extreme externalizers will most likely get into trouble or have physical symptoms with their behavior. Extreme internalizers, on the other hand, tend to suffer emotional symptoms such as depression and anxiety.

Internalizer or externalizer traits can be beneficial or can be a liability depending on the situation. Internalizers, for instance, are prone to self-defeating tendencies such as inaction and avoidance of seeking help. On the other hand, externalizers may live a messy life but due to their impulsive style, they are more willing to act and try various solutions. Such impulsiveness is sometimes exactly what is needed in some situations, and on such occasions, it can be considered a strength.

In the right situations and conditions, each of the coping styles can be useful and problems often occur for people who are at the extreme of either coping styles. Despite this, the overall externalizer profile still shows a personality that is less adaptive and unrealistic and this is primarily because their emotional immaturity simply does not allow for successful relationships and does not promote psychological development.

In Summary

Children react to emotionally immature parenting in different ways but they all subconsciously create healing fantasies that things will get better. A child will also develop a role-self so as to have a valuable role to play in the family if his true self is not accepted by the family. Furthermore, when responding to emotionally immature parenting, children develop either of two main coping mechanisms which are externalizing and internalizing. Internalizers look within themselves to solve their own problems but the externalizer believes that the solution to their problems will be from outside themselves.

Chapter 6

Being an Internalizer

Internalizing children who are very perceptive will easily notice when their parents are not connecting with them. A less aware child cannot register emotional hurt the way that perceptive internalizing children do and so are less deeply affected growing up with emotionally immature parents. Internalizers are sensitive to the subtleties of relationships and so are greatly aware of the loneliness that occurs as a result of emotionally unengaged parents.

Internalizers are Very Sensitive and Perceptive

Internalizers are very sensitive and do notice a lot of things far more than most people. They have been prompted to be attuned to other people's feelings and needs by their senses. This perceptiveness can be both a burden and a blessing. Internalizers could have had an extremely alert nervous system from birth. Research has demonstrated that differences in babies' environmental attunement and perceptiveness can be observed at a very early age. This also dictated the kind of behavior exhibited by the children as they grow, this thus shows a possibility that a predisposition to a particular coping mechanism exists from early childhood.

Internalizers have Strong Emotions

Emotions of internalizers tend to intensify because they are bottled in and not immediately released or acted out like in externalizers. Internalizers can often be seen as too emotional or just overly sensitive because they feel things deeply. They tend to cry when they experience something painful and some parents just can't stand this due to being scared of emotional displays. Conversely, externalizers act out any strong feelings they experience before they can experience any internal distress. Most people will likely view the externalizer as having a behavioral problem instead of an emotional one while not being aware that emotions are the root of the problem.

Emotionally immature parents can punish externalizers for their behavior but will instead dismiss an internalizer's feelings with contempt. Internalizers are sometimes told that their very nature is their problem while the focus is placed on the behavior of the externalizer.

Internalizers Have a Deep Need for Connection

Internalizers are sensitive to the quality and genuineness of emotional intimacy in their relationships because they are attuned to feelings. They strongly desire emotional intimacy. Internalizers need to share their inner experience; their desire for a real emotional connection is a great part of their existence. For internalizers, nothing hurts more than being around people who cannot engage them emotionally, it is not a social urge for them but rather a strong hunger to connect on a more intimate level with like-minded people who can understand them and when they are unable to make this kind of connection, they feel lonely emotionally.

When children who are internalizers have self-involved or emotionally unengaging parents, they do think that being helpful and neglecting their own needs will win their parent's love. However, being counted on does not equal being loved and the emptiness of this strategy becomes obvious. Despite that, these children still believe that to make a connection, they need to put other people's needs before theirs and treat others as more important. They believe that by being the giver in a relationship, they can sustain it but they do not know that conditional behavior cannot get unconditional love.

Internalizers Have Strong Instincts for Genuine Engagement

Have you ever given thought to why feelings of disconnection and isolation are stressful? Is it that it is simply less pleasant to be alone or maybe there is something more to it? Why is an emotional connection so crucial? It was not so surprising to know mammals can reduce the physical effects of stress by seeking contact with others. Stress hormones and heart rate can be reduced by comforting gestures such as touch, eye contact, soothing sounds, and physical closeness. These effects calm and also create social bonds.

Understanding That Connection is Normal, Not Dependent

Internalizers should view their instinctive desire for emotional connection as a positive thing, strength instead of as a negative, seeing it as being too dependent or needy. Turning to others for succor when stressed makes people more adaptive and stronger. These emotional needs show that their instinct for seeking comfort is healthy and functional. Instinctively, internalizers do know that there is strength in being interdependent, this could be seen in the popular saying: "strength in numbers". Seeing wanting understanding and empathy as a sign of weakness is characteristic of emotionally immature people.

Forging Emotional Bonds Outside of the Family

Children who are internalizers tend to find sources of emotional connection outside of the family because of their heightened perception and a strong need for emotional engagement. They are aware of when people respond to them warmly and so they seek relationships with these people outside the family to have a greater sense of security. Internalizers can get emotional nourishment from resonating with art and nature. They can also embrace spirituality to give the emotional nurturing they strongly desire as they relate to a greater who is always with them.

Externalizers similarly have needs for emotional comfort but they instead take other people emotionally hostage by forcing those needs on them. Most times, externalizers use their behavior to manipulate certain responses from people but due to them achieving these responses through manipulation, it is not as fulfilling as a genuine exchange of intimacy. People who have been blamed or guilt-tripped by externalizers end up feeling forced to help and this can lead to a build-up of resentment.

Relationship between Emotional Immaturity and Avoiding Engagement

Emotionally immature people are externalizers who are unable to reap the benefit of genuine emotional engagement and calm themselves. When experiencing bouts of insecurity, they feel threatened and stressed and instead of seeking comfort from people launch into flight, fight or freeze behaviors that are commonly observed in reptiles. They tend to react to anxious moments in their relationships by resorting to rigid, defensive behaviors that result in other people being alienated rather than being connected to. Externalizers have poor skills in reaching out to people for soothing and comfort and they display domination, blame, anger and criticism.

When externalizers get upset, it sometimes seems like they have a strong desire for emotional engagement but this approach tends towards panicking instead of connecting. It requires a whole lot to make them calm but despite that, they still remain dissatisfied because of their inability to connect fully.

Physical Survival: The Role of Emotional Connection Skills

Having a strong drive for succor through genuine emotional connection has benefits that surpass merely making people feel better, it can literally save lives. Getting reassurance and support from close relationships can help people to survive extreme and life-threatening conditions. If fight, flee or freeze up behaviors are a person's only coping mechanism during stress, then it will be very difficult to endure a lengthy challenge. Research has shown that people who survived impossible situations lived through such circumstances by calling upon their present relationships and the memories of those they love as a source of strength and will to survive. Basically, everyone needs a sense of genuine intimate connection to feel fully secure and there is nothing wrong with that.

Internalizers are often Embarrassed about Needing Help

After finally seeking help, internalizers are mostly apologetic and feel undeserving of receiving such help. Internalizers who grew up in a family with emotionally immature parents are often surprised when they find out that their feelings are being taken seriously. They downplay their emotional needs and some even believe they shouldn't get therapy because there are people who need more help than they do, this indicates that they most likely grew in a home where externalizers were the only ones who were helped.

If shamed for showing their sensitive emotions as a child, when they become adults, they may become embarrassed to display any deep emotion. They can apologize for crying in a therapist's office when talking about their emotional problems. They are oftentimes convinced that displaying their deepest feelings means that they are inconveniencing other people. When people show genuine interest in the feelings of an internalizer, they often become surprised and are caught off-guard.

Internalizers Become Invisible and Easy to Neglect

Externalizers are very easy to spot in a family, they are the kids who get annoyed over the simplest matter, the teenagers who keep getting into trouble and the adult children who cause nothing but problems. Externalizers are always at the top of their parents' concerns. Parents with externalizer children tend to devote more time and energy to them than to other children.

Internalizers on the other hand, often appear to be getting on just fine and do not need much attention or nurturance as the externalizers because the internalizers instead rely on their own inner resources. Internalizers are often afraid to ask for help and often times resort to solving their problems on their own. They are often low-maintenance kids who do not require much attention and are very easy to overlook. For preoccupied parents, self-reliance may precipitate emotional neglect.

Emotionally immature parents believe that their internalizing children are able to sufficiently take care of themselves and so they allow them to have an independent life outside of the family. Although internalizing children can be independent and cope successfully, they still desire to capture the interest of their parents and connect with them. No child deserves to be emotionally invisible and especially not highly emotionally attuned and sensitive internalizers.

Getting by on Limited Recognition

When growing, internalizers that are emotionally neglected continue to feel as if they have to do everything on their own and then they become more adept at doing this. Internalizers are able to assimilate whatever they get from others because they like to learn and remember experiences. Internalizers also have an excellent emotional memory and will and they reach within themselves when they are not getting emotional nurturance from others. Internalizers often take on so much responsibility for other people without much thought and so are very grateful for even the tiniest bit of recognition and this is one of the specific characteristics of an internalizer.

Recognizing Childhood Neglect

When parents are emotionally immature, it is

guaranteed that their children will suffer emotional neglect. This deprivation, however, is silent and is an invisible experience for these children, they will feel emptiness but they will not know what name to ascribe to it. They will grow up like this and still not be able to identify or realize that they are suffering from emotional loneliness but they will feel different from those who truly seem at ease.

People often do not realize that they are suffering from or have suffered emotional deprivation until they read about it for the first time. The self-sufficiency of children who are internalizers often creates the impression that they have no needs. They are expected to be okay without anyone looking out for them or carefully watching over them. They are often referred to as "old souls" and their parents trust them to always do the right things.

Learning to Ignore One's Feelings and Receiving Only Superficial Support

When children have had to become tough and learn to do things on their own, they can develop an attitude of rejection towards their own feelings. It is likely that they have learned to keep away from those painful feelings which their emotionally immature parents cannot help them with.

Neglect can also occur in the form of emotionally immature parents giving such comforts that do not really help the scared child in any way.

Internalizers are Overly Independent

It is possible for emotional neglect to make premature independence to seem like a virtue. A lot of people who suffered emotional neglect as children do not often realize that their independence was not a choice but a necessity. Children who have been independent may not learn how to seek help when they grow up even when such help is readily available. Psychotherapists and other counselors have the responsibility of coaxing these people to accept help by making them see that their need for help is legitimate.

Internalizers do not See Abuse for what it is

Internalizers are unable to recognize abuse for what it is because they look within themselves when things go wrong to seek for the reasons that things went wrong. If parents do not see their actions as abuse, the child won't recognize it as such either. As adults, internalizers still do not have any idea that they had been abused in their childhood and as a result, they still do not recognize abusive behavior in their adult relationships.

Internalizers do Most of the Emotional Work in their Relationships

It is not surprising that internalizers put in a lot of emotional work into their relationships. Emotional work includes using self-control, empathy, and foresight to get along with others and to foster relationships. Parents do most of the emotional work in healthy families but when the parents are unable to cope, an internalizing child will step into the gap created by such parents and such a child can become overly responsible.

Adapting Compensatory Cheerfulness

Internalizing children can take up a cheerful role so as to bring liveliness and happiness, especially when parents are depressed, into a melancholic family climate. With their good sense of humor and liveliness, they try to help others to feel that things are not as bad as they seem.

Doing Emotional Work for Parents

Emotionally immature parents will avoid emotional work at any opportunity they get and so may not deal with their children's emotional issues or attention problems, thus leaving the children to work through it on their own. Emotionally immature parents are unhelpful when their children need emotional support, they may be dismissive when their child expresses his feelings of being hurt. Internalizers, due to their natural sensitivity, do emotional work for their parents and sometimes, internalizers play the role of emotional support before they are old enough to do so.

Overworking in Adult Relationships

Internalizers are used to supplying most of the empathy in their relationships and they often believe that they can be able to single-handedly love someone into a good relationship. Since they do most of the work in trying to get along with people, they become worn out without noticing that the other person is not changing at all. Internalizers are so used to providing the sensitivity missing in their family members and they automatically do this with everyone, they sometimes take up emotional slack in their relationships by playing both parts of the interactions and act as if there is reciprocity when in fact there is none.

Internalizers often end up in unequal relationships despite doing their share of the emotional work because needy externalizers are more likely to go after warm and giving internalizers, they can initially make the internalizer feel special so as to secure the relationship and when that has been accomplished, they stop reciprocating. The internalizer, however, believes that they are to blame for this change in the relationship.

Attracting Needy People

Emotionally immature people cannot resist relying on self-contained internalizers because these internalizers seem so strong and do not require help or support from anyone else. Internalizers are perceptive and sensible and this makes even people that they have met before trusting them. Needy strangers will take up a sensitive person's time and attention at the slightest chance they get.

In Summary

Internalizers are extremely sensitive and very

perceptive of other people's needs. Growing up with emotionally immature parents is very painful for internalizers because of their strong desire to connect emotionally with someone. Internalizers are prone to be emotionally neglected by emotionally immature parents because they refrain from bothering other people with their "strong" emotions. They create a healing fantasy that makes them believe that they can change other people's behavior and feelings about them while also developing a role-self that's totally focused on other people. Internalizers do a lot of emotional work in their relations and even end up doing too much while they can get by on very little support from other people. When internalizers do too much emotional work in their relationships, they can become exhausted and even start to harbor resentment.

Chapter 7

The Dusk Before the Dawn

Most of the time we are the master of an ill-fitting role because we have been in it for so long. The details in this chapter explain how people feel when they wake up from what they have been doing wrongly. The awakening stage is characterized by the presence of both physical and psychological symptoms such as depression, anxiety, sleeplessness, fear and severe tension. When these symptoms set in, then we should be certain that we have been getting it wrong for a long time.

True Self

According to the studies carried out by psychologists among different populations in the world, it is believed that the reality of true self is that it is similar across culture. Its concept is that it is viewed as being moral and good. True self is considered to be as old as the "self" itself and can be attributed to the time a person was born. Sometimes, our true self can also be referred to as inner self, real self or core self. In most cases, what we find ourselves doing is contrary to what our true self craves for and yet we keep doing it. Each person has a unique personality and the interesting aspect of the true self is that it cannot be manipulated by the pressure of the environment, families or even the way we act.

Sometimes, all we care about is how people perceive us which leads to not knowing the exact person we are and it gets to a stage that all we want to do is please people. You know your true self when you are conscious and aware of who you really are. True self isn't the other self you wish to be, rather, it is the exact person you are. The connection we have with our true self makes us see things as they are and feel more relaxed that we are on the right path. When we pay more attention to ourselves, we tend to be luckier as more opportunities come to us and also people will want to be associated with people that are real.

The Demand of True Self

Like every attribute that we have, your true self doesn't want to be hidden; instead, it wants to be expressed.. The main thing it demands is for you to eliminate negative thinking patterns and replace them with a positive and supportive mindset. Your true self wouldn't be satisfied with your current situation but it will always encourage you to be better and fulfilled in a more genuine way. Most times, it is not interested in whatever the ideas that crept into your head while you were younger. The true demands of your true self is for self-actualization of dreams through sincerity and honesty. This act makes your true self feel happier, successful and fulfilled.

Children are usually influenced to be their true self

when the adults around them encourage them to do so. They become in charge of their thoughts and tend to expose more of who they really are. But when they are made to know life is all about bringing out your false self instead of your true self, pretense sets in and all that matters to them is how they can please their parents and others in order to be loved. They deny their needs and desire while they turn off their true self and tread the path others lead them to and in the process, play a role that isn't theirs.

There are a few things you can engage in to activate your true self.

Exercise: Waking Up Your True Self

This is one of the greatest adventures you can undergo in your lifetime. When you ignore your deepest needs, your true self ignites your emotional being to remind you that you have to take care of yourself. When you are aware of these emotional symptoms you get when you are drifting from your true self, you bounce back to who you used to be then you see things as they really are.

The aim of this exercise is for you to awaken and be conscious of your true self. Wakening to your true self might be a wild thing to explore but it is better for you in the long run. The materials required are a piece of paper and a pen. Fold the paper into two equal halves so that you can only use a side at a time. Write a heading which says: "My Role Self" and "My True Self" respectively on each side of the paper.

Start with the heading "My true self". In this case you have to be truthful and honest with yourself while you reminisce on your childhood days. Children are mostly influenced by the people and the environment they grew up in and are identified by the defenses of their parents which affects the expression of the real personality of the individual. This stage requires being brave and willing to remember the things you did in the past, those things you cherished and the things you were comfortable doing. Remembering these things takes you through the road of having a deep understanding of who you are and what you really stand for. Other things to put into consideration in the past include the things you enjoyed doing, the things you were good at, the type of people you loved to associate with, the reason you moved with them, what made you grow fond of them and the type of sport you enjoyed playing (indoor or outdoor). These analyses should be done without the consideration of money as it may be a <u>confounder</u>, which can stand against honesty. When you have written the necessary things, move on to the next page.

Write the heading "My Role Self" on the next page. This phase acts like a self-assessment which is required to provide information on your personality and who you have grown to become in the past years and is a justification for the recent way you act, what are the attitude you have put up in order to be loved and appreciated. Do the things you do make you happy or do you do them primarily to please people? Do you feel comfortable with the people you have around you?

what are the things you do and do they interest you or bore you? Do you care more about what people say about you than what you feel about yourself?

At the end of the assessment, put the piece of paper aside for some days, after which you open it up and straighten the paper. Then compare both sides and assess yourself. Are you fulfilled and do you do what your true self desires by checking your role self or do you do what is contrary to your true self?

Breaking Down To Awaken

When people live outside their true self and the influence of their role self reduces, they begin to experience breakdown. Psychological growth can be affected by how we have been expressing ourselves and it can be either frustrating or fulfilling depending on the path you choose. Sometimes we go through breakdown and everything that comes to our mind during this period is self-pity. It is not a bad idea to feel sorry for oneself but in most cases, that should not be the first resort. The first thing you should entertain in such situation is to know the cause of the breakdown. When we think forth, we resolve to the fact that we are responsible for the breakdown when in the real sense, it is caused by the inability to keep up with the emotional lies which brought us down rather than the truth that could have held us up. There are varieties of things that can break us down but for the context of this book we will consider emotional unconsciousness and distress.

When you begin to feel emotionally unstable with the acts you have put up and it seems you have broken down, then you should know that your true self is wanting to find a way to creep out. Your true self starts by waking you up and letting you know that the emotional immaturity of your parents will not give you the best life you desire. Rather, you have to free yourself and find out your true self-ignoring who you have been made to believe you are.

According to Jean Piaget (1963), in order for people to hold on to new things, their initial belief of the thing must be allowed to break up and rework itself for the knowledge. The process of breaking down and waking up helps you discover yourself. Kazimierz Dabrowski (1972) believed that emotional distress should be viewed as a sign of growth and not illness except in few cases.

Sarah's Story

Dabrowski's ideas gave Sarah the strength and courage to be a better person. Sarah believed she used to be a woman of value and integrity and known to always be happy. However, challenges came and she had difficult choices to make. In no time, she became a shadow of herself and all she cared about was what people thought of her.

When Clara her old time friend discovered she was not the person she grew up with, without her consent fixed an appointment on her behalf. At first, Sarah was mad at her friend for thinking she had psychiatric problems but Clara succeeded in luring her to respect the appointment.

At first, Sarah felt she was doing the wrong thing by going to the therapy but her friend felt she needed to get back to who she used to be. At a stage, she knew better based on her awareness of parent's immaturity, avoidance of emotional intimacy and impulsivity. But how could Clara have come across the exact thing she needed and how does she knows she needs help?

Dabrowski's idea on positive disintegration was the answer to Sarah's doubts. When she had the knowledge of Dabrowski's theory, she was grateful Clara was helpful and glad she accepted the assistance.

Awakening From Playing Role Self

For how long can people play the role-self game, maybe into adulthood but never for too long. There comes a time where you wouldn't feel the need to impress people or to go out of your way so as to be accepted. When you feel like this, then you have gotten a wakeup call which comes alongside emotional symptoms. The change can be quite obvious and sometimes unaccepted by your immature parents.

Rhoda's story

Rhoda's wakeup call was quite different from others as she felt attacked and scared when she was confronted by her brother Brian. This wasn't the first time she was confronted which makes the sudden panic attacks a surprise to her. Rhoda has always felt like a stranger and an unlovable person especially by her parents, which was the reason she swore she would go any length to win her father's love. However, this never happened until he died and then her brother arose to the same act. The challenges she had with the mixed roles she had to play in her family influenced her relationship with other people. Rhoda began to worry constantly about what people thought of her and became scared of rejection.

When Rhoda's panic attack surfaced she began to feel uneasy and reminisce on her childhood belief that people who are older than her are usually right especially men. She confessed she usually feels scared and frightened whenever people express their displeasure towards her. The panic attack made her see her relationship with Brian more clearly "he was treated like a god". He never cared so much about her, yet his opinion mattered the most to her and her life revolved around the things he wanted. Rhoda confessed, "I have never been happier since I was born especially knowing that I can be myself".

The panic attack opened her subconscious mind to what had been closed to her since her childhood days. She felt she no longer needed to accept the story of infallible male as she had done since childhood.

Exercise: Release Yourself from a Role That Is Self-Defeating

Grab a note pad and write a short and precise description of a person in your life who makes you feel anxious or affect your self-esteem. Then, write down how you feel and act when you are with that person, do you feel you are yourself with the person? or do you pretend to get along well with him/her? Do you wish this person would act differently towards you and for how long have you been expecting a change? Are you willing to let this person know your true self and the way you want them to treat you?

Waking Up To What You Really Feel

Sometimes we find ourselves accepting what we wouldn't give room for on a normal day. We feel guilty for the things that are unacceptable to our true self. We have believed that the only way to impress people is to accept every stone they throw at us. However, if we suppress our feelings for a long time, we eventually turn to take a look at what is wrong.

Rachel's Story

Rachel was raised by a single father whose wife eloped with another man after a year of Rachel's arrival, which means that she barely knows her mother. Her father Koffi, had to relocate to the united Kingdom to avoid the embarrassment his wife caused him in the neighborhood. Singlehandedly, he raised his daughter trying as hard as possible to provide her with virtually everything she needed. Rachel felt the only way she could show appreciation to her father for the love, affection and sacrifices he had made for her was to be who he wanted her to be and of course make use of every educational opportunity that came her way.

During the course of her hard work, she earned herself a fully funded scholarship for her advanced degree. She felt she needed to go for therapy when she was at the verge of completing her advanced degree due to depression. She had to struggle to move on in life even though she was allowed to work; she had no zeal to do anything productive.

After many interrogations, her depressive mood was known to be related to the kind of relationship she had with her father. Being a single father, he was overly protective and kept reminding her about the incidence that brought about their relocation. In every conversation, he mentioned how far away he was from his family and friends. The main point here is that he didn't allow himself to heal from the occurrence. Rachel felt bad and tried as much as possible to develop hatred for her mother at the expenses of loving her father. However, listening to her father's misery only made her sympathetic and sad.

I knew what she must have gone through, she felt bad she couldn't help her father in the situation but felt worse that he wouldn't stop talking about the incident. Deep down, she already developed hatred for him although she tried to control it but it was all to no avail. As the complaint persisted, she became depressed. When she accepted the fact that she hated him, the therapy took another shape and it was as if she let go of a heavy burden she had been withholding for a long time.

She convinced herself that she didn't like her father

although she would always be indebted to him for the care and help he rendered her. She knew at that instance that she couldn't hide her feelings forever; else she would lose herself in the process.

Exercise: Exploring Whether You Have Hidden Feelings

There are times you feel anxious and down for no particular reason within your reach. The truth is that there is a reason behind whatever you feel. Check yourself and consider if you are holding on to anything or anyone that's making you have such feelings. Another thing that can be helpful is for you to remember when you had such a feeling and relate it back to the things/persons that prompted such feelings.

If a person is responsible for the feelings, write down your feelings in a very simple and clear manner. You can do this privately to avoid distractions and other people's influence on your decision. Then in a polite manner, speak to yourself about what you don't like concerning the person. Is it the way the person addresses you or the way you feel the person treats you? When you voice those things out, you feel better and release the tension that has built up.

It's not compulsory that you confront the person concerning his/her act. The goal is for you to feel better and not embark on a hatred journey. Confrontation can come later when you feel better and have a free mind concerning the person.

Waking Up Through Relationship Breakdown

Experience in the world of psychotherapy has made me realize that relationship problems are a major wake up tool. Being that we display painful patterns which we were taught during childhood into our adult relationships. When we do not get our emotional needs met, they become unresolved issues. In intimate adult relationships, sometimes we project our parent's issues onto our partners and unconsciously, we become angry with them.

Michael's story

He sat down to think of how much his life has crumbled after losing his job and his wife filing for a divorce for a twelve years marriage. Everyone had thought he was at the top of his game and he was having a fulfilled lifetime and he believed them.

When things came crumbling, he decided to give therapy a chance before he finally went insane with the happenings around him. Thinking deep down, he realized he had been living a major part of his life to please people. He endured a marriage that lacked love and saw the whole thing crumbling and then he felt like a failure contrary to what he had thought initially. As he reflected on his past, he could boldly say, 'I am glad all the setback occurred, they are my source of inspiration'. When he was asked about his next pursuit on success, he responded 'success can wait. Firstly, I have to know me'.

Waking Up from Idealizing Others

Most cultures make us believe parents know better or even in the real sense they are wiser. This unproved theory was only backed up with age. Even when children become adults, the environment does not make them acknowledge their mistakes and weaknesses. Sometimes, it is obvious that they are wrong but the idea we have grown to believe is that their mistakes should be endured not pointed out because all of their acts can be justified. Unfortunately, it is because we don't want them to feel vulnerable but the truth still stands that they cannot always be correct.

Waking Up to Your Strengths

When you think of working on your weakness, you should also appreciate your strength. However, children brought up by immature parents have a contrary experience of such. Their positive qualities are usually not dwelt upon or appreciated because such parents do not have the ability to see the strength of their children. This has resulted in making the children embarrassed of every quality they possess.. They are used to encouraging the good qualities of others and feel it is wrong for their own strength to be pointed out.

The fact that your parents do not see your strength doesn't mean you shouldn't see it either. Identify your good qualities and embrace them. Know what you stand for and the positive virtues you possess. However, to stand in the phase for a long time, you have to be honest and modest in everything.

Waking Up to Forget Childhood Issues

Consciously or the other way round, we have had childhood emotional injuries. Realizing and working through these emotional injuries is a way of waking up and healing. According to a study by Cassidy et al., it is found out that parents who raise kids that are securely attached are always willing to talk about their own childhood. Although some of them do not have pleasant childhood experience, however, they made their children feel secure. These parents know what it feels like to have emotional injuries and will do their best to ensure their children do not face the same dilemma.

Chapter 8

Being Free From Emotionally Immature Parents

When we were children, we had so much confidence in our parents that we saw them as semi-god. You can blame it on childhood because we believed they could never be wrong. The more we grow, from the stages of adolescence to adulthood, we know better but this belief is not permanently eradicated. All of these occur due to beliefs and some things we have been made to believe even when the contrary is occurring in our presence.

Some of the beliefs include:

- Only your parents genuinely want the best for you
- Even when you trust no one, your parents should be an exception.
- Your parents love you
- Parents are wiser
- They will always be there for you
- You can trust their advice
- Everything they tell you is true

All of these are true as parents are amazing but when your parents are immature then all of the statements cannot work for you. This chapter aims to help you know your parents and guidelines on how to relate with them without losing yourself in the process. There are unreal beliefs that a parent will change.

The Unreal Belief That A Parent Will Change

When children feel unloved by their parents, they feel incomplete and do all they can to make them have a change of mind. But in most cases, the anger they vent on the children is not due to the way they act, as children are lovely but rather it can be the circumstances that surrounded their birth or they want to make up for their own childhood hurt. When you view it from this aspect, you will agree with me that changing their heart is a lifetime fantasy.

On the verge of trying to gain their parent's heart, children go as far as hopping around them and trying to please them at any given opportunity. This zeal isn't curbed by adulthood, rather, they keep hoping and trying their best.

Betty's Story

Betty was raised from what was far from love. Her mother, Tracy whom people see as being a kind and generous person abused her at every opportunity she got both physically and emotionally. Although, Betty was used to this treatment, she always yearned for better treatment and always wanted to feel the mother and child bond. Betty reached her breaking point when her mother made a <u>derogatory</u> comment about her in the presence of her friends. She felt hurt and embarrassed that she couldn't face her friends for a month, then her self-esteem dropped to the lowest. She decided to take things up with her mother and confronted her. Tracy didn't give room for such conversation and her silence only made things worse. So, she resolved to writing to her with the hope that it would help but all to no <u>avail</u>. The gap began to grow wider and Betty knew she needed to confide in someone before it got out of hand.

Betty grieved on how much she wanted her mother to love her and how hard she tried. The most confusing thing is the difference in the way she relates with other people and with her own daughter. "Betty" I said, you have tried all a person can do but you did the right thing following the wrong step, considering the kind of relationship you mentioned occurred between your mother and grandmother, you should be pretty sure, she is trying to vent anger on you. Yes, you will think after all she had gone through in the hands of your grandmother, she should have treated you better but she isn't happy the way she is treating you but she hasn't healed from the emotional injury she sustained with her own mother. I told her the only way Tracy can ever consider a relationship with her is by not complaining of her attitude towards her, rather she should make decisions that doesn't have to do with her consent. She will come around with time but you should not make the effort to change your parent.

Isolated Observation

Checking out everything you have read in this book, you already know how to identify immature parents. Think of your parent that falls into this category and act your own true self to them as its less probable that you will win them over as a loving parent.

Family system theory which was proposed by Murray Bowen in 1978 gives an insight on how immature parents create emotional enmeshment over their children true self. Parents who are immature do not have genuine conversations and intimacy with their children. Such families are better referred to as housemates. Bowen further explained that when parents tend to cause emotional injuries into their children, rather than the children sitting to mourn, such children should indulge into other things that make them happy without losing themselves in the process.

Become Observational

You can only have a peaceful conversation with immature people when you allow yourself to feel calm and relaxed. So being observational is a practical act not a theory. You can start by detaching your frame of mind and being observational rather than trying to prove a point because you might not win. Do not allow emotions to be in charge of your attitude towards them. Do not be bothered by what they say, rather think of something else, travel far and wide in your mind and win yourself over instead of allowing them to disturb your heart.

When you discover you are already reacting to their words, detach your mind immediately and, in your mind, go over how that person has acted towards you in the past. That way, you will look at them as whom they really are without having to prove a point to them. From the moment you are feeling you can't take it anymore; find a way to excuse yourself. Go to a place you can feel relaxed and distracted. Your observational acts will keep you strong and make you be yourself rather than the person people have defined you as.

The Maturity Awareness Approach

This approach helps you to consider the emotional maturity of others when you are dealing with them. You categorically estimate the maturity of the person you are dealing with in your head and it gives you an insight of how you should relate with them.

You should deal with emotionally mature and immature people differently. Here is an aid on how to deal with people that you consider emotionally immature without hurting yourself.

- Communicate and let go: Express yourself in a calm and polite manner and turn a deaf ear to the result

- Keep the relationship away and focus on the result: Be sure of the need for the conversation and don't be involved in a conversation that requires the changing of the mind of your parents. Let your

communication come with a goal that is feasible to be achieved.
- Cope and do not engage: The interaction should be precise and the time should be well managed. Do not give room for emotional conversations that would hurt you.

Changing An Old Self Role

Your emotional freedom can only begin when you do not just consider your parent's maturity status but also examine your attitude if you are your true self or you play a role self. When you have seen where you play the role self, then you are a step ahead and all that is required of you is to change your role and do what you feel is best for you.

Minding Your Feelings And Thoughts

When you are able to control your own thoughts and feelings, then it will be easier for you to interact with immature people. To do this, you have to begin by being observational, you should adopt the maturity awareness approach. With this act, you will develop immunity to whatever is thrown at you and you will be calm even when blame is directed at you.

When you are dealing with parents having predicted the outcome of the conversation will help you keep calm as you already have an idea of what their response would be.

Be Cautious Of Changes in People

According to Murray Bowen (1978) "as a child becomes more of an individual, the emotionally immature parent's knee-jerk reaction is to do something that attempts to force the child back into an enmeshed pattern. If the child doesn't take the bait, such parents may ultimately start relating in amore genuine way".

You need to be careful when your parents show unusual openness especially when you just adopted your observational approach. Once they start doing the things you have been pleading with them to do, be careful not to get trapped or lured into being your old self. Keep tabs and let's see how long it will last before you fall into the trap. Your inner mind would be glad that you have succeeded in winning the heart of your parents but you should let them know you aren't changing your true self. If you fall back and trust their changes, you might be disappointed.

The truth is your parents will want to come closer when they feel you are drifting apart. When you operate from your renewed mind, you will keep the gap while they do the changing if it is genuine. Never forget to keep observing and be true to yourself. You shouldn't lose yourself for anything or anybody.

In Summary

While we were young, we depended so much on our parents and we saw them as superhuman who we must always please. Yes, they deserve to be pleased but only when we are \doing it for the right reasons. We have to know the things we need and how we can get them. We should assess the maturity level of our parents and how we can relate with them if they are immature. Emotional injuries should not be sustained into adulthood.

Chapter 9

Living Free of Roles and Responsibilities

In this chapter we take a look at how life could be different if you start living a life free of roles and responsibilities, when you start living your own life and not a life meant to please an emotionally immature parent.

Family Patterns That Could Be a Source of Hindrance to Your Growth

Before we explore ways of living a life free of roles and responsibilities, it's important to look into the patterns that could be holding you back from living your life for yourself. Some of them include:

Disapproval of Individuality

If you were raised by an emotionally unstable or immature parent, chances are that you spent your young life walking on egg shells. Rather than being allowed to be yourself, express your opinion, act your natural self, you are forced to mirror their actions, thoughts, opinions and lifestyle even if they go against what you believe in or the way you would want to speak or act. An emotionally immature parent due to their own insecurities and fears prefer the predictable kind of life that you have been taught.

These parents are scared and threatened by their children's individuality, they are afraid when their children express themselves or act in their own best interest because it breaks the predictable pattern they are used to. Therefore, the children in turn rather than making their parents anxious because of their actions and words, would rather suppress their individuality and pretend to be who they are not, just to give their parents a sense of security.

In such cases, children are often ashamed to express the following emotions:

- Spontaneity
- Enthusiasm
- Grief/sadness/sorrow
- Expressing their innermost thoughts
- Affection

On the other hand, they are taught something else entirely and these include:

- Absolute obedience to authority
- Physical illness that allows the parents exhibit their authority
- Self-doubt
- Liking what the parents like and vice versa
- Shame over being imperfect
- Ability to listen to their parents complaints and distress

- Stereotyped gender roles and responsibilities

If you have an emotionally immature parent and you were an internalizing child, then you would have been taught a lot of self-defeating things which ought to help you get along in life. Some of these things include:

- First consider what others want from you
- Never speak up for yourself
- Don't ever ask others for help
- Be satisfied and don't ask for more

Internalizing children have been taught by their emotionally immature parents that 'goodness' is synonymous to being self-effacing and that their parents demands must be met first before anyone else. They see their desires and feelings as unimportant or shameful. However, once they come to see it for what it is (a distorted mind-set) then it becomes easier to set things right.

Sticking To an Internalized Parental Voice

You may wonder how it's possible for parents to train their children to go against their gut instincts or feelings but this is not only possible but is natural. Sometimes, when we find ourselves wanting to do something or take a particular action, there is that inner voice echoing in your mind. Now while you may think this is your inner voice speaking to you, it is the voice of your early caregivers talking through a process called parent-voice internalization. This voice may make unkind comments concerning your self-worth, intelligence and character.

The fact is that everyone internalizes their parents voice, while some are lucky to have been brought up by very supportive and friendly parents and hence have positive parent-voice internalization, others are not so fortunate and so have pessimistic parent-voice internalization. However, there is a need to break out of this pessimistic parent-voice internalization as only then can you truly know your self-worth and not judge yourself based on their critical evaluation. The aim is to identify the voice as a foreign language and not part of your own thinking, and this is done by using the maturity awareness approach already discussed in chapter eight to relate with the negative voices just the same way you will use same approach with your parents.

The more objective you get about your emotionally immature parents, the more you also have to reevaluate the voices in your head and start detaching yourself from their unnecessary influence. Again, just as your parents, you also need to observe how these internal voices speak to you and then you can take it with a pinch of salt and make a rational decision on whether you want to keep listening to those internal critics.

You are Free to Be Human and Imperfect

It is most likely that internalized parental voice gets its origin from the left hemisphere, a region where language and logic is dominate and when this left brain is allowed to do its job, it chooses efficiency and perfectionism before feelings, judgment and compassion (McGilchrist 2009). Without the right side of the brain which is the personal and intuitive part, your left brain is like a machine which uses the equation of right and wrong to assess you. It will inform you when you are good, bad, broken or perfect and this is done according to your achievement. This kind of assessment is an aspect of mental rigidity that is associated with emotional immaturity.

You Are Free to Have Genuine Thoughts and Feelings

If you were raised by emotionally immature parents who are not comfortable with your thoughts and feelings, you would have learnt how to suppress such emotions. While growing up, knowing your true thoughts and feelings probably felt dangerous to you especially if it threatened to push you away from those you were dependent on. You were wired to think that you being good or bad is not only in what you do but it's in your mind too. You may also have been trained to believe that you can be a bad person simply by having certain thoughts and beliefs.

However, there is a need for you to have access to your inner experience without the feeling of shame and guilt. In addition, you will have more energy when you allow your thoughts flow in a natural pattern rather than worry if your thoughts are good or moral. A thought or feeling is nothing more than what it is and allowing your thoughts and feelings to come and go as it pleases is a huge relief.

If you must know, you mostly do not have control over

your thoughts or feelings, you simply think or feel, it's just a way of nature expressing itself through you and there is nothing to be done about that than to allow it flow as it should rather than suppress it. When you accept the truth of your thoughts and feelings, it doesn't mean you are a bad person, it only means you are whole and that you are mature enough to know your own mind.

You are Free to Suspend Contract

I am certain you will like to have the freedom to be yourself while also protecting yourself when it comes to your relationship with your parents. Yet, there are times you will need to suspend contact even if it's for a while in order to save your emotional healthy. This is likely to stir up self-doubt and guilt but when you consider what you stand to gain by doing this, and then there will be no room for guilt. There are parents who are hurtful and disrespectful of their children's boundaries and even after repeated explanations as to why it's not acceptable, they still don't get it, perhaps because they relish being difficult or perhaps because it's the only way they know, either way in such situation it's necessary to keep your distance for a while.

Fortunately, you dont have to have an active relationship with your parents to get away from your parents, people are able to live very far from their parents and move on when they die just because they are your parents does not mean you have to keep a physical or emotional tie to such people especially when they are toxic.

You Are Free To Set Your Limits and To Choose How Much You Can Give

While suspending contact is effective, some people are also able to set limits and stick to it such that their parents do not have the avenue to do them more harm. This can be done by limiting the frequency of your contact with them. When you set limit on your contact with your parents, you are then able to dedicate more time to your self-care. You may feel guilty and selfish at first, however, this time gives you the opportunity you may have for choosing yourself and your mental health over your emotionally immature parents.

You Are Free To Have Self Compassion

It is said that in order to take good care of yourself, you must feel compassion for yourself (McCullough et al. 2003). Feelings and sympathy for oneself are the basics of strong individuality, without this you will not know when to set limits.

When you are sympathetic to yourself, you experience a form of healing although this may seem unnatural at first. One woman found her old school picture, in it she was smiling despite what she was dealing with, "what a strong girl you were" she said to the picture. When you are sympathetic to yourself, you may feel grief and tears and that's normal too, Daniel Siegel has so much to say about the healing power of emotions in his books (2009)., tears are sometimes needed to feel better.

Regaining the ability to feel compassion for oneself can come in intense waves as having a lot of unprocessed emotions can be a bit overwhelming. Reach out to a compassionate friend or a therapist to help you through this process. Allow your body to grieve and cry when needed, let your feelings arise and continuously try to understand them, when all is said and done you will emerge a more mature person who has great compassion not just for others but for herself too.

You Are Free Not To Be Excessively Compassionate

One of the problems of being an internalized person is that such people can feel excessively compassionate for other people's problems; they tend to end up feeling worse than the person perceived to have the problem. What is needed is a healthy empathic feeling, this helps you be compassionate and yet not lose focus of your own limit.

You Are Free To Take Action on Your Own Behalf

If you grew up with emotionally immature parents, there's the tendency of you feeling helpless as though no one can help you and that you don't deserve to be helped, unless someone offers that help at their own discretion.

It should be noted that such upbringing can be very traumatic and can transcend to your adult life such that you have feelings of not being able to do anything or not deserving of help, you may feel like a victim with no control and at the mercy of others who may not want to give what you crave for.

However, you can regain your freedom from this kind of feeling no matter how ingrained in you it may seem. You can take action on your own behalf as this is the antidote to the feeling of helplessness. It's true that emotionally immature parents do not give you a good picture of what life and relationships have to offer, but it is my hope that you are starting to realize that your possibilities are endless and that you owe yourself a duty to ask what you want.

You Are Free To Express Yourself

When you express yourself with emotionally immature parents, it's a form of self-affirmation and an assertion that you exist as an individual with your own feeling and thoughts. Its important to let go of the thought that if your parents loved you, they would understand you, you may never have that kind of relationship with them and that's ok, what you need to focus on is making sure that each conversation with them is satisfying for you.

You are free to speak politely, to express yourself without having to make excuses. When you express yourself to them in this form, then you are being your true self even if they do not understand. The main point is to be authentic and not to change them, also note that it's possible for them to love you even when they do not understand you.

You Are Free To Approach Old Relationships in a New Way

You have the freedom to converse with your parents in a new way and shake up their old patterns. They may react in a more emotionally genuine way or they could become worse but then they may open up more when you stop wanting them to change. When they see how strong you have become without the need for their approval, they may begin to relax. If you stop expecting them to change, then chances are that they will be able to accept more openness.

This will only happen when you stop expecting them to change or act in a certain way and even at that, these changes may not occur at all no matter what you do. However, its important that you stay true to yourself, to stay emotionally detached and to expect nothing from them. When you expect nothing from them, you give them the freedom to be their true selves while you on the other hand also maintain your true personality.

You Are Free To Expect Nothing from Your Parents

With emotionally immature parents, the pain comes when their parents need something from them. It could be love, attention or communication, many children tend to feel neglected and continue to feel so even at adulthood even when it's clear that their parents are incapable of giving these things.

They have trained their children to believe that they are the only source of self-esteem and well-being for their children, they love it when their children are needy and dependent on them, it gives them a sense of control and fulfillment and if given the chance they completely have control over their children's emotional state.

However, you must realize that you are free to want nothing from them. You need to step back and ask yourself if you really need them. The truth is that if they were not your parents, they may not be the sort of people you may require anything from. So, it's best to consider if you really need anything from them.

It's important you ask yourself these questions as it helps you know where you stand as most times you are just swept into believing you desperately need your parents when you actually don't.

In Summary

In this chapter, we delved into what it feels like to live a life free of roles and responsibilities and how it feels to break away from these roles which are meant to please emotionally immature parents. No thanks to your internalized parental voice, you may have learnt to reject yourself and to be critical but we have looked at ways of breaking that chain and reclaiming your true self regardless of how others may feel about it.

You are free to express yourself, take actions on your behalf; you are free to extend compassion to yourself, to grieve and cry and not bottle it all in, you now realize that your first responsibility is to yourself and that if need be you have to set the limits and boundaries. You also now know that as you expect nothing from your parents and allow them to be their true self rather than try to change them, they too are free to be their own genuine self no matter what the outcome may be.

Chapter 10

What is an Emotionally Mature person

In this chapter, we will look at ways of identifying emotionally mature people, those who are mature enough to engage in a beneficial relationship. I will also be sharing with you how to adopt new attitudes about relationships as this helps you to put emotionally immature people in their place.

Most often, grown children of emotionally immature parents are skeptical of any relationship as they don't belief that a healthy relationship can enrich their lives. They have the underlining fear that people will not be interested in what they have to say or who they are. These negative emotions depict emotional loneliness, which can be changed once you are aware of them.

The Mystique of Old Pattern

John Bowlby (1979) said "all humans share the primitive instinct that familiarity means safety".

It is therefore safe to say that if you grew up with emotionally immature people then you are most likely attracted to the familiarity of exploitative and egocentric people. Research has shown that most girls are more attracted to the bad boys than the nice ones, the good ones are considered boring which is to say that if the boy isn't arrogant, selfish and dominating then he's not attractive.

But this makes one wonder if this is really appealing and exciting or if it's just a reflection of their childhood anxiety coming to play in their adult life, what really makes an adult want to be involved in what is clearly not good for them? According to the schema therapy developed by Jeffery Young (Young and Klosko 1993), it stated that we are usually subconsciously attracted to those who trigger us to fall back into negative and old family patterns. He admonished that this kind of instant attraction for bad things is a danger sign, an indication that the self-defeating roles we were used to in our childhood are being activated beneath the surface.

Identifying People of High Emotional Maturity

This section offers some guidelines that will help you identify emotionally mature people after which rather than subconsciously make decisions or stick with people who damage you or bring you down you can make a conscious effort to choose those with the positive traits outlined. Whether you are choosing a career, going into a relationship or friendship, you can make use of the characteristics discussed to identify those with a long-term relationship potential even if it's online. They don't have to get it right 100% as no one is perfect, however, you will be sure of having an enriching relationship with this set of people rather than one that drains you. These characteristics include:

Emotionally Mature People are Reliable and Realistic

Realistic and reliable may sound humdrum, but nothing beats someone with this foundation. It's just like a house, the color doesn't matter, what matters is the structure of the building for without a firm foundation the house falls like a pack of card. The same applies to a healthy relationship; a good relationship should feel like a well designed house, easy to enter and exit without much thought to the planning and architecture put into it.

Emotionally Mature People Work With Reality Rather Than Fight Reality

These sets of people are constantly working to change the things they don't like, but are always aware of reality in its own terms. When problems arise, they try and fix rather than overreacting or obsessing on how things should be and if things aren't working out a planned, they just make the best out of the situation.

They Think and Feel Simultaneously

An emotionally mature person is able to think even when upset and that's someone you can reason with. These people have the ability to reason with other people and see a different perspective even when things aren't going as planned. They are focused and don't loose track of emotional factors when they are addressing an issue.

They Are Consistent, Hence Reliable

These people will not spring inconsistent surprises on you as they have an integrated sense of self, they are predictable to an extent and can be counted upon to be the same in different situations. They can be trusted as their consistency makes them so trustworthy.

They Are Not Overly Sensitive

Emotionally mature people are not so touchy and don't take things too personally; they can laugh and take a joke even if they are the subject of such jokes. They are realistic enough to know they are not perfect, hence they see themselves as infallible even while doing the best they can.

People who take things too personally are either people with a low self-esteem or a narcissist, these traits are not healthy as they constantly lead people to seek validation from others. This is not all, they also tend to think they are being evaluated at every given point and see criticisms where they are not, and they are always on the defensive.

They Are Respectful and Reciprocate

With emotionally mature people, everyone is worthy of respect and are treated fairly, they have a corporative orientation which is evident from all the traits they possess and in how they treat others. They give you a feeling that they look out for you rather than being focused on their own self.

They Respect Boundaries

Emotionally mature people are very courteous, respect and honor boundaries. They are in search of connection and not invasion. These people do not assume that since you love them then you love what they love too. Rather, they take your feelings and desires into consideration; they are in tune with how others feel. Though this may seem like a lot, but to them it's as natural as breathing in air.

One of the attributes of a healthy relationship is one in which you are not told what to do or how to feel. If you grew up with emotionally immature parents then you are probably used to unsolicited advice and analysis from others. This is usually the case that in themselves have problems and are looking for ways to use others to make themselves feel good. Rather than stick with these kinds of people, its best to migrate to those who respect you for who you are.

Emotionally Mature People Give Back

Rather than take advantage of you, emotionally mature people are generous and always want to help out, they are generous with their time while at the same time asking for help when they need it. They are always willing to give more than they get back but in all they do they try to create a balance between things.

With emotionally immature parents, they have trained you to either give too much or too little, they are always demanding and this will have an effect on you in the long run. If you grew up an internalizer, you would believe that to gain the world's approval you have to keep giving and giving despite being drained or getting nothing in return.

They Compromise

These people try to be fair, objective and flexible. One of the traits to look out in people with whether or not they are emotionally mature is how they respond to change in plans. You should watch out if these people can't differentiate between a rejection and a sudden change of plans. Are they able to express their disappointment without trying to blame you? if a situation comes up and you can't stick to plan will they understand, will you be given the benefit of doubt? Will they be empathic and compromising?

Emotionally mature people are aware that disappointments and changes are a normal phenomenon in life, rather than dwell on their disappointments they look for alternatives and solutions; they are open to ideas and won't blame you for what you have no control over.

Rather than have you bring it all, they meet you half way while the reverse is the case for emotionally immature people who always pressure others into concessions that they alone stand to benefit from.

Other Attributes of Emotionally Mature People

The list of positive attributes of emotionally mature

people are endless, some other attributes which they possess include:

- They have an even temper
- They don't mind being influenced
- They don't lie
- They don't hesitate to apologize and make amends
- They are responsive
- You are safe in their empathy
- They see and understand you
- They comfort and like to be comforted too
- They are optimists; laughing freely and being playful
- They are fun to be with

What to Look Out for When Meeting People Online

The traits described in this chapter are also applicable to those of social networking and online dating. In fact, it will interest you to note that online gives you the platform to identify emotionally mature individuals as people can reveal so much about themselves simply by their profiles and their messages.

It true that some people are better writers than others, however, all personal writing reveal what people really think and feel, the things they value and what they are focused on. You can also detect if they have a sense of honor or not and whether or not they are sensitive to other people's feelings. In addition, reading messages from people gives you time to reflect on how they make you feel.

Whether it's a phone call or messages give yourself time to think of how that person's timing and pacing makes you feel. Do they respect your boundaries, how fast or how slow are you in getting to know each other? Are you being pressured into intimacy or are you uncomfortable with the person's tone? Do you feel as though such person is placing too much hope on you even before getting to know you or are they slow in responding or do they always want you to be the first to reach out? Are they empathic, reciprocal? Do they acknowledge your opinions and insights or do they always want to have the final say? Do you both agree and schedule things to fit each other in or are you constantly out of sync with them?

When you are done viewing a profile, reading an email or a message or receiving a phone call take a moment to write down your impressions. This will help you focus on your gut feeling and this is easier as you are not pressured into a physical communication. While writing, describe how you feel, this will help you identify if such a person is emotionally mature.

In Summary

In this chapter we looked at ways of identifying emotionally mature people and the attributes they possess. We also looked at new ways of relating with people that can help you create a more satisfying relationship with them. From all that has been discussed, I am certain you can now identify emotionally mature people and with that new knowledge, you will no longer be tempted to settle for less. You are now able to look for the traits you want and keep searching until you find those with such traits and with this come a healthier and more fulfilling relationship with everyone.

Conclusion

It's not always a pleasant experience to dig up your past even if it's with a view of understanding and shining light on the things that happened in order to be better.

A light is meant to illuminate everything it touches; it does the same with your past too. When you decide to shine a light on your past and discover the truth about not just yourself but your family relationship and how it has affected your life, you will be shocked at what you will discover especially when you realized the patterns that are now playing out in your own life, a pattern that has been passed down from generation to generation. You may question if it's even worth discovering and if it has any effect on your present life.

Well, the answer to this lies in what value you place about life and whether or not you consider your discoveries important enough for you.

You are in the best position to answer this question as no one else has the answer but in my experience I have observed that self-awareness comes with a deeper connection with oneself and with the world, when you work through your difficult past, it makes your present more real and precious. Moreover, when you come to understand yourself and your family, only then are you able to appreciate your life like you have never done before.

When you recognize and resolve your frustration and confusion about emotionally immature people then you are able to live a richer and happier life, you will also feel lighter. It is my hope that this book has helped you not only know yourself and your loved ones more but it has also brought about freedom to live your own life based on your own terms and your own genuine feelings and thoughts rather than that of others.

You must recognize that people rarely change unless they want to, so rather than waste your time trying to change what cannot be changed, focus on yourself and change yourself, choose the path of happiness and self-awareness. You don't get to live your life twice, so you may as well make very good use of the opportunity and live it right.

Your life is yours, live well, and live happy.

Narcissistic Fathers

The Problem with being the Son or Daughter of a Narcissistic Parent, and how to fix it. A Guide for Healing and Recovering After Hidden Abuse

Dr. Theresa J. Covert

Introduction

Growing up, did your father ever make you feel unheard and rejected, like your emotions, thoughts and wants never mattered? If yes, there is a high likelihood you were raised by a narcissist, and I can empathize with you on that one. I had a childhood where I was not allowed to do things that made me happy. Being myself, expressing myself, following my passions and voicing my opinions equaled punishment. My father was a narcissist too and it is the narcissistic abuse that I experienced that got me into psychology in the first place.

We can't choose our parents, nor our surroundings when we are born. A child who is raised by someone who has an NPD is, from a very young age, deprived of very basic things necessary for establishing one's identity, having healthy boundaries and self-esteem. These basic things are as simple as genuine love and care for a child's needs, approval of their identity and support, and that is exactly what a narcissist can't provide. Instead of preparing their children for adulthood, narcissistic fathers sabotage any attempt of authenticity. There are very few things that can damage the core of one's self as being raised by a person who classifies as such. Exposure to constant gaslighting, and living with guilt and shame from a very young age, leaves deep scars on a child's psyche and follows them into adulthood until they gain enough consciousness and awareness to heal and reinvent themselves. Many of us who grew up in a toxic environment found it difficult to be authentic and even worse, we thought we were the ones to blame for not being good enough, successful enough or a good enough child. Such children frequently become highly anxious and afraid of the world around them from a very young age, afraid of everyone's judgment, of confrontation, voicing their opinions or saying no to unreasonable demands. Some seek love and validation in wrong places as adults and many feel less-than, even when they are extremely talented, smart or likable.

Fortunately, the great majority of children, now adults, who grew up in love-deprived homes and were raised by a narcissistic father, find ways to heal and reinvent themselves to become authentic individuals throughout life. What was repressed for such a long time, eventually finds expression through self-work and therapy. Such a childhood poses a barrier to personal development and many feel remorseful once they figure out their parent is a narcissist. And that is ok. It is one of the first steps to healing and it is acceptable to be remorseful. After all, this book is all about that, accepting who you are, embracing all your feelings and thoughts, even the bad ones, and then learning to gradually, at your own pace, let them go.

Even nowadays, there is a stigma around breaking free from family chains. The ugly truth is, not all parents are good parents and you don't have to be grateful to your parents if they mistreated or abused you, physically or psychologically. This content is meant to help you break free from guilt and shame carried from a relationship with a narcissistic father. Hopefully, it will provide you with some guidance, shed light on who you were dealing with at their core and learn more about their effect on you. It is meant to help show you how to accept your family history as part of your journey, not your final destination, nor perceive it as chains you can never break free from.

If you are a child of such a dysfunctional father, you probably know what it's like to feel never good enough, even if you are more successful than most of your peers. You probably know what it's like to feel invisible, rejected and anxious from a very young age and you might be far too familiar with how hard it is to even try to voice your thoughts and emotions. Maybe you are a late bloomer like my sister, who was so afraid of becoming true to yourself and independent, only because being codependent is the only thing you've known. And maybe you rebelled against your father's concepts early on and became a black sheep in the family, like me. Whatever your story is, childhood colored by someone's narcissism leaves scars on self-esteem and deep-rooted fears and patterns that make us sabotage ourselves later in life. We are afraid to say no to things that don't serve us and yes to a great job offer because we think we don't deserve it. Both my sister and I spent a childhood, teenagehood and early adulthood feeling guilty for everything and anything, feeling unsuccessful, not talented or beautiful enough, like who we truly were wasn't acceptable. Being raised by a narcissistic father took a toll on both of us, but in a different way. Although we were raised in the same family, we received entirely different treatment. Feeling like a disappointment is not easy, especially if it follows you your whole life. It was a tough road on which we learned to trust ourselves to make decisions, voice our truths and feel good about who we are. Narcissists discard the very essence of their children. They don't teach them to speak up and be self-sufficient, but to stay quiet and obedient.

Know this - you are not alone. You'd be surprised how many people I have met, who, just like you and me, didn't feel good enough because that is what they were made to believe their whole lives. Although not an easy path, because change doesn't happen overnight, a path of recovery from long-term narcissistic abuse, such as parental narcissistic abuse, gets easier with every step you take. I ask you to be gentle with yourself and allow for a change in you to occur as you get ready for each next step. It gets better. Much better. Recovering from narcissistic abuse is something that will make you see how strong, loveable and capable you are and always have been.

Chapter 1

Who are narcissistic fathers?

Paternal narcissism relates to fathers who display behaviors typical of narcissistic personality disorder. Narcissistic fathers have grandiose delusions related to self, one's importance, abilities and talents, and they impose superiority, are malicious, manipulative and controlling. In dealing with others, they lack empathy, are extremely self-centered, possessive and arrogant, and when it comes to their children these behaviors become even more highlighted. In the core of a narcissist's mindset is a very fragile ego, which revolves around unrealistic fantasies of grandiosity and self-importance. They use family bonds to fulfill their narcissistic desires. Having such a parent creates an emotionally unhealthy environment for a child and leaves long-lasting consequences on their mental health. When such a dysfunctional individual is a parent, the very person a child depends on becomes the greatest source of instability, anxiety, depression and low self-esteem for the child.

Outside their family life and father-child bonds, they are often highly charismatic, charming people and frequently are very successful, well-accepted members of society. A narcissistic father is someone who needs to feel important and in control of everything around them, including the life of their children. They are the people whose rage is hard to deal with, who guilt-trip their children and punish them by withdrawing love, money or other resources children depend on. A parent with an NPD is the type of person who would take away whatever it is their child cares about, be it their favorite toy, forbidding them going out or refusing to support their aspirations. While all parents are protective of their children, in this case, what lies behind such behavior is pure self-interest and a need to protect their narcissistic supply, even if that means doing something that is not for the greater good of the child. More so, the narcissist feels completely entitled to being the center of the family dynamic, demands obedience, respect and won't accept any form of rebellion against their demands and wishes.

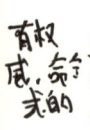

While many narcissistic fathers are the overly-authoritative type, narcissistic behavior is not always displayed as openly threatening, especially with the less domineering, covert narcissist. Individuals who display behaviors typical for NPD gaslight, play mind games, act resentful or passive-aggressive, use other's empathy, loyalty and emotions to manipulate them and gain narcissistic supply. They use other weaknesses to make themselves feel important, grandiose and respected and sadly not even their own children are spared. On the contrary, narcissistic fathers perceive their children as their "property", an extension of themselves or a project, making their children feel like they "owe" them their time and obedience even later in adulthood. Such children are expected to live the life their fathers expect them to live and live someone else's dreams (read: their father's).

Highly unsympathetic and insensitive to the child's needs, these fathers withdraw affection, don't respect the child's independence, and are unable to form truly loving bonds with their kids. These children aren't allowed to be their independent selves, or have their own lives, and so fighting for independence and personal authenticity is a constant battle, which it never is in healthy father-child relationships. Their aspirations, goals and dreams never matter and there is no room for being a unique individual. The identity of a child is built to suit their narcissistic parent and match their father's expectations. A narcissist will do anything and go to great lengths to try to mold them to fit their ideal image of a perfect child who admires them - "you must be what I want you to be, or...". They will do so under the parole "I know what is best for you", but the reality is, a narcissist only knows what is best for themselves and that is to keep their narcissistic supply close to them at any cost.

Paternal narcissism also often includes marginalization of the child, dismissing their personal uniqueness and even a competition with the child - competition for recognition, admiration and adoration. Fathers like these need to take the center stage at all costs. Usually, they will live the success through the child and their accomplishments, so they may be the first one to brag about their child's latest accomplishments and make great celebration parties, only for them to be seen and admired by others as a good, accomplished father.

Conversely, they will be the ones to criticize and put the child down if anything a child does threatens to crumble their false sense of grandiosity.

In their mind, being a father gives them power over their children, and they think in terms of entitlement to power: *you depend on me so I can decide what you can or can't do with your life.* They need to give approval, permission or consent of everything the child does, from the beginning, because a child's independence threatens this exact false sense of control and power. Furthermore, they need to be in control and puppet their child to be a good representation of how good of a father they are, as it serves their ego and raises their status.

I hope this book will help you break that toxic chain. Us who suffered narcissistic abuse in childhood are those who need to re-educate and re-parent ourselves. And that is a journey we should be proud of with every step we take.

Chapter 2

Signs of a narcissistic father

A narcissistic personality disorder is characterized by a sense of entitlement, a false belief that one is grandiose, a need for admiration, adoration and a lack of empathy. There are two main types of narcissistic fathers, and both exert these characteristics. They are overt narcissists and covert narcissists, where the first may exhibit more personal dominance, arrogance and extreme resistance to criticism, the second type is more shame driven and less extraverted in their approach to others. Nevertheless, both are toxic and malignant to be raised by, and their behaviors and patterns can easily obstruct the child's growth, causing them mental health problems in adulthood, creating identity crisis, codependency and self-confidence issues. When distinguishing a narcissistic father, there are a few key ways in which one can determine the presence of narcissism. The most important ones to take notice of are a father's attitude towards the daughter, the dynamic of their relationship and their parenting style towards a single child. Narcissists see all their children differently, so it is important to compare the father's relationship with all children separately, as it is not uncommon for them to have a golden, favorite child and prefer one over the other. If you are suspecting your father exhibits traits of a narcissist, here are a few major signs to look for to help in discernment:

A narcissistic father is either overly involved or completely detached. Their involvement in their offspring's life varies from complete possessiveness to absolute indifference, depending on how a child is behaving and their own narcissistic disposition. They are overly involved in all aspects of their lives, from school or university life to socializing, hobbies and dating. Narcissists are self-centered people, and they take their children's success and failure as if it was their own, which will additionally dictate their involvement or noninvolvement. If they are proud of their child, they will make sure the child and themselves are seen, if not, they will completely ignore and disengage themselves from their child's life as if the child is not deserving of love just for being who they are.

They see their children as extensions of themselves. That being said, their children are not seen as individuals, but parts of themselves, which causes the father's and child's identities to merge. Because of that, everything a child does is taken very personally, be it for good or for bad. Every success is seen as a personal success., It boosts their self-confidence and is an affirmation of their own value. Conversely, every perceived failure and mistake a child makes is subconsciously seen as their own fault. In such situations, a narcissist can even rigorously punish the child for embarrassing and disappointing them. The affection between them is present and the nature of such a relationship is a codependent parental relationship. Instead of attending to the child's actual needs and paying attention to their individuality, such fathers live through their children. They pay attention to similarities between themselves and the child and diminish or even punish what makes the child unique and authentic. The father lives through the child, and so they focus on their potential, rather than the real capabilities and desires of a child.

The father idealizes the child. Idealization takes many forms and is based on the father's unrealistic perception of the child, where he exaggerates and tries to boost certain aspects of a child's personality while taking no notice of other aspects. He always has an image of a perfect child in mind, a child who is successful in all areas he'd like her to be successful in and will go out of his way to boost, praise and amplify skills and personality traits he finds to match this idealized image. It is not uncommon for such a father to ignore the child's natural talents and gifts if they do not match his projected ideal. They will push their children into hobbies and activities they personally prefer, not those the child is the most interested in. Every behavior that is compatible with idealized images will be loudly praised, while everything that deviates from that will be ignored, punished, sabotaged or dismissed.

The narcissistic father is overly controlling. Because they are driven by the idealized image of their child, the parental relationship is colored with an extreme amount of control. The father needs to be involved in every decision-making process and needs to have a firm grip on every aspect of their child's life. This includes schooling, career choice, time, hobbies and leisure activities, choosing friends, socializing and dating, personal appearance, money or anything else they can have control over. An excessive amount of control is there to ensure two things: One, to establish a solid narcissistic supply and create a child's dependency on them, and two, to prevent a child's independence and detachment from them.

The father ignores the child's emotional needs. Due to a lack of empathy and the inability to connect with others in a healthy way, children of narcissistic fathers are frequently deprived of true affection, which leaves marks on their emotional self later in life. They are not allowed to say or express how they feel and the free flow of love and affection is interrupted by the constant cycle of pricing and shaming. As a result, such children learn that love is never given freely, but must be earned, which is what the emotional bond between the child and the narcissistic father is built on. Love is always conditional and kids are not loved for who they are, but for who their father wants them to be. Such fathers usually shift the focus to building their child's skills, manners or preparing them for success, completely ignoring their emotional wellbeing. This is why, even though a father may be a present figure in the family, when he is a narcissist a child may feel rejected, neglected and ignored due to his inability to tend to their emotional needs or give nurturing care, just as if he wasn't there at all.

The father displays superficial charm. Narcissists are very charismatic people and like to be admired. They know the right things to say or do to be liked and well received by people. For someone who is not in close relationship with them, a narcissist will appear very pleasant, sociable and respectable. To the outside world, they seem like great dads, who sacrifice a lot and always fight for their family, which can cause confusion in their children - *Is my father really as manipulative as I believe? Maybe he is really trying to help me. Maybe the problem really is me. Am I not allowing my father to guide and protect me?* A child of a narcissist will often hear how great of a father they have, and that they should be thankful for having someone so attentive to raise them.

Narcissistic fathers are easily triggered and enraged. Narcissists do not tolerate criticism or failures. Because they don't have a well-developed emotional intelligence, they display almost infantile reactions to behaviors and situations they don't approve of. Internally, when they feel ashamed, undervalued, rejected and afraid, they will project these negative emotions onto other family members, including a child. These reactions, or projections, can vary from passive-aggressive treatments, insults to outright rage. Because of their mental disposition and idealized picture of how things should be, they do not accept deviations from expected perfection. Human faults and mistakes are seen as disasters and something a child should be ashamed of, not something they can learn from or something that could contribute to their personal growth. There is a lack of compromise, flexibility, and adaptability to other people's needs, including their own children, as a narcissist truly, deeply believes everyone else should adapt to them.

The father makes a child feel guilty and ashamed. A child grows up feeling as if there are parts of themselves that need to be hidden, parts of their personality that are not acceptable and should be kept in control, including a child's emotional nature, aspirations, interests, and talents. These are usually not naturally deviant behaviors by any means, but simply behaviors that deviate from their father's idealized image. For a child, there is usually an unexplainable element of restriction and extreme awareness of one's behavior from a young age, followed by a sense of not having enough freedom to explore, be spontaneous or creative as a child. Furthermore, there is a sense of fear that being authentic will incur the father's judgment and rejection. Growing up, a child is deemed guilty by their father for not trying harder, not doing better in school, not looking or behaving better, or not behaving as good as their brother, sister, relatives or neighbors.

A narcissistic father played the blame game. They have an inclination to blame everyone else in the family when they experience personal failure or have issues, be it the other parent or the child. Lack of admiration, recognition for their talents and capabilities, lack of success or bad health are always because of someone else. *Your mother never gave me enough love. If it wasn't for your mother, I would be the main engineer right now. If it wasn't* *for your university debt, we would have bought a new house. If it wasn't for your brother's disinterest for a family business, we could have grown the business. If it wasn't for your bad behavior, I wouldn't have heart problems now.* A narcissist believes the whole world is against them and everyone tries to sabotage them, so family members are usually at fault when their self-perceived talents and value don't get the recognition they think they deserve. Due to grandiosity complex, they don't take responsibility or accountability for their failures or behaviors, but simply pass them to a scapegoat - a person who is blamed for the narcissist's mistakes.

Paternal narcissism is very complex, but these fathers all display these behaviors to a different degree. Not all narcissistic fathers will be the same in their relations with children, but all of them will have some of the listed elements combined together. Hopefully, these signs were helpful and could give you some clarity about what you've lived through and who the person is that raised you. First recognizing and accepting that your father may not be the protector you thought them to be is the first step to understanding some of your own patterns, behaviors and most importantly, it is the first step to building yourself up and healing from such a relationship.

Chapter 3

The dark core of personality in narcissistic fathers

Some of the questions I commonly hear from survivors of parental narcissistic abuse are: *Why did my father treat me the way they did? Couldn't they be a better parent? Maybe I am asking too much. Maybe I am selfish. Maybe I am a failure. Maybe I am spoiled. Didn't they love me? What did I do to deserve that? I must have been a really bad child. I am disappointed after all.* These and similar questions naturally awaken resentment, anger, the deep sense of injustice and, not uncommonly, self-blame and even self-hate. After all, no one deserves to be put down and marginalized, especially not by the people they couldn't choose, such as their parents. Asking these questions and feeling every human emotion is ok and it is normal. This is what you need to know - whatever you experienced as a child was not your fault.

Along with Machiavellianism, sadism, egoism and spitefulness, the psychology of a human mind can include another dark trait that relates to lack of empathy and consideration for others - narcissism. Belonging to this spectrum of dark elements of one's personality and a very complex personality disorder on its own, narcissism at its core is extremely toxic for a narcissist's environment. This is to say that narcissists aren't mentally and emotionally healthy individuals and can't provide the same nurturing as healthy fathers would.

A narcissistic personality disorder is characterized by a certain level of emotional infancy. Because they haven't learned to accept and reciprocate affection in a healthy way and because of their lack of empathy for others, they have instead learned to rely on other aspects of personality to survive in society - their intellectual capabilities, physical strength, power, and charisma. They do feel very powerful emotions, but these emotions are usually fear and anger on the negative spectrum, and feelings of worthiness and self-importance on the positive spectrum. Both emotions on the positive and the negative spectrum drive them to do things that would result in someone validating their worth. Their sense of personal happiness, after all, depends on that. More so, narcissistic fathers, as narcissists in general, are fiercely driven by their own fear, and the fear they awaken in others.

Furthermore, there are two main types of narcissism, and these are grandiose or overt narcissism, and vulnerable or covert narcissism. Fathers who belong on the grandiose narcissism spectrum are likely to show behaviors such as dominance, extreme self-confidence, insensitivity, lack of consideration for others, insensitivity to their needs and authoritarianism. They openly demand to be the center of attention, desire admiration, love to brag and are frequently in the spotlight where he loves to be. Those who belong on the covert spectrum, however, are inhibited in their displays of grandiosity. They too believe they need to be admired and have a false sense of grandiosity and an inflated ego, but these fathers, compared to overt narcissists, will be more passive-aggressive, appear more vulnerable and sensitive to criticism. The base of the personality, however, in both cases remains the same. Both types lack empathy and both believe they are special, have an inflated sense of self-importance and dream of being adored, and having ultimate power and control. No matter if your father is a covert or an overt narcissist, you are likely to experience rejection, feelings of unworthiness, feeling unlovable or less-than. The psychology behind narcissistic behavior is such that these people have a sense of entitlement and crave external admiration, which in combination with a lack of care and empathy for others, can be disastrous for their children.

Are feelings of being deemed as unworthy of love and admiration, untalented, unsuccessful, not good enough, and the fear of possible failure something you are experiencing as an adult or something you recall from childhood? All of these are fears are very common for survivors of parental narcissistic abuse. The irony here is that all these fears, however, are exactly the fears a narcissistic father has at his core. These exact fears drive them to manipulate, lie, gaslight and put their children or partners down, only to feel powerful. The narcissistic personality is a mix of extremes, a mix of fear, of not being seen for one's great value, and an obsession over that illusionary value.

Narcissists have tunnel vision and perception of reality, which revolves around superiority and very fragile ego - a bo explode any second you do something th ...nes to ruin their illusory world. The emotional self of the narcissist isn't built on equal give and take, as they believe they should be the ones to have it all, which is why the relationship between them and the child revolves on conditioning and conditional love. Emotional satisfaction from a father-child relationship, as well as in other relationships in their lives, is established by interpersonal dominance and exertion of some form of power, through arrogance, authoritarianism, manipulation, gaslighting, blaming or lying.

Furthermore, narcissists project aspects of themselves onto their children, which because of a child's innocent and gullible nature, easily finds a way to their behavioral patterns. I spent my teenage years and early adulthood feeling the extreme need to succeed and impress everyone because I wanted to prove to everyone that I am worthy. I thought I needed to be perfect in order to find a good relationship and be respected, but the only thing that brought me is misery, anxiety and depression. In my mid-twenties, when everyone was still discovering themselves, I felt like a failure and disappointment. I really wanted to make my father proud of me. I wanted to prove him wrong and make him see and appreciate my talents and who I am as a person. Narcissistic fathers set criteria for your iness and because we are talking about childhood, these criteria get very deep-rooted in your psyche as if it was your own. This creates a deep inner conflict and a struggle, to the point, it is even hard to discern who you are and what you really want out of life, without the father speaking through you.

Chapter 4

Narcissistic fathers and their inability to love

Part of the mental disposition of a narcissist is the inability to reciprocate healthy emotions without an agenda attached. A narcissistic father's love is a selfish love. Because they can't truly feel such an emotion, the love given to the child is always conditional: *I will love you only if you do as I say and behave the way I expect you to behave, no matter how you feel.* Nothing is free and every action has consequences, and so when a narcissist gives, you better believe it is because they want something in return - a validation of their grandiosity. A narcissist only shows attention and shows displays of love when it suits them, to ensure the child will give them back twice the amount of that displayed love. Like in any other type of relationship with a narcissist, there are three main stages they put you through, and these are love bombing, devaluation, and discard. Because of the unique nature of parent-child relationships, in this case, while growing up a child strongly experiences the first two phases, which are closely entwined and don't happen in a particular order. The discard usually happens when a child completely rebels against their fathers' wishes and demands and becomes an outcast that deserves nothing else but to be completely rejected and deemed as unworthy of their father's love. There is a constant swing between being the perfect, golden child and a disgrace and disappointment for the family.

Because a narcissistic father doesn't see their child as an individual, but rather an extension of themselves and a source of narcissistic supply, they give their love based on how well the child fits into that image. If a child is the artistic type and would like to pursue a career in the arts, and their father's dream is for them to become a lawyer, the child will feel guilty for pursuing their own dream. Even though they may be a very talented artist with a lot of creative potential, they won't have the support they need. Matter of fact, they may even be punished for going after the goals and aspirations that make them happy because the only person whose happiness matters is their father's. In a healthy father-child relationship, love is given freely and is a catalyst for personal growth and prosperity in the family. However, in a malignant relationship, the love a child has for the father is used as a tool, a weapon for manipulation and control.

Every time the child does something that feeds the ego of a narcissist and approves of their power, such as listening to their advice, obeying their rules and doing what they find is acceptable, they will get love bombed. Love bombing involves extreme praise, displays of affection and rewards. These are not just any rewards, but those things the father knows the child highly cares about and craves for, be it time spent together, financial support or something as simple as the freedom to do their hobby and stay out later than usual. During this stage, a narcissist will say things that make you feel special, valuable, seen, heard and appreciated, something every child needs from their parents. In these moments you feel very worthy of love and get much-needed confidence as they assure you that you are so perfect you could conquer the world.

Love bombing serves to ensure the narcissistic supply and it is so effective because what lies behind it is a calculation based on careful observation and studying of their child. They know what the child needs to feel happy and fulfilled, what their dreams and hopes are, and so the narcissist will use it to derive the desired behaviors that make themselves feel good - *I have the power to make you feel worthy or unworthy of love.* While a healthy parent will do anything in their power to protect their child, help them build strengths and deal with weaknesses, a narcissistic father preys on their child's weak spots and vulnerabilities and uses them against the child. They know how you react to love so they know how to serve it to you, and they know exactly what they will get in return. By giving the child the power to make decisions for themselves, the narcissist feels unimportant, which causes them to rage, and projects such feelings of personal inadequacy on the one who made them feel so powerless - their own child. As a result, it is the child who feels unappreciated and powerless. Although his words may sound genuine, at the core of his being, he doesn't care about the child's wellbeing, happiness or who they are and want to become. Behind the mask of a father who only wants the best for their child is a selfish, smart manipulator who needs everything to revolve around them and doesn't care about family and family matters, unless they feel threatened. Love is never free-flowing, and the child feels obligated to return the love, idealization and praise. The child will repay them by obliging the narcissist and giving their undivided time and attention, whenever the narcissist demands that.

Discard happens when you, as their child, fail to do what they want and then you are seen as a disgrace and a disappointment. You deviated from the plan of how they want you to be, you don't play the role in society they want you to play and this means you are unworthy of love and support. They will punish you for doing anything willingly and without their consent, by withholding things that matter to you, such as hugs, time, devotion or money. You will be ignored simply for having your own opinion or saying no to something that isn't in your best interest. Cold treatment, passive-aggressiveness, criticism and back-handed comments are something I grew up with. This would make me crave the praise and affirmation I had during love bombing moments and amplify the feeling of unworthiness even more. I would feel extremely pressured to answer my father's calls, do him favors and try harder to be a better daughter, only to end up feeling guilty for not making the man who raised me, my father, proud of me. I used to think I deserve love only when I put others first, as I was so used to letting myself down and trying to please someone, who never had my best interest at heart. I would later learn that pleasing them kept me small and brought me nothing more than anxiety, shame, and guilt I did not deserve.

Chapter 5

Weapons of a narcissist: How a narcissistic father controls

I hope previous chapters gave you a clearer insight into what a narcissistic personality is and helped you define paternal narcissism. If your father is a narcissist and his behaviors match plenty of those that were previously described, you may start wondering how come you did not recognize them as a narcissist for so long. Many children, who are now adults, whose fathers are narcissists, that I've met deny and second-guess themselves even after there are plenty of signs pointing out the existence of narcissism in their fathers. They wonder if they are simply overreacting, as after all there were so many positive memories with their father they could recall. This is because they, just like me and you, were raised to second-guess themselves. Second-guessing and mistrusting one's own judgment are part of being a child of a narcissist. Narcissistic fathers are masters of manipulation and disguise. They are masters at creating positive memories, as these allow them to control your behavior. There are a few common ways in which they manipulate and control. Some are more prevalent in grandiose narcissism, and some in vulnerable narcissism, but all narcissists use all of these techniques to an extent, some more than others. All of these techniques are damaging to a child's self-development, self-esteem, identity, emotional, mental and even physical health. They are so damaging because parents are the first role models in everyone's childhood, narcissists or not. The first conditioning and the first contact with society for a little child is through them, which is why children naturally see their parents as the ultimate protectors, the good people, the people who teach them how to love. When a parent is a narcissist, the very dynamic of a family becomes unhealthy and the child grows up in a toxic environment, not knowing or understanding why they are treated the way they are. The very first contact with society is through them, so a child who was raised by a narcissist won't be able to label parental behavior as toxic or abusive until they grow up to understand the devastating effects their father left on their very core of personality.

Narcissistic fathers frequently marginalize and criticize their children. This makes them feel more secure and in power, but it also makes the child more vulnerable to them and more insecure. To feel special, the child in return wants to feel like they matter, and they seek their father's validation by doing exactly what the father wants them to do. Because the father is a respected figure a child trusts, like we all do, especially when we are young, the first thing that comes to a child's mind when they are criticized is that they are somehow bad, that there is something wrong with them, or that they are doing childhood wrong.

My father used to compare my sister and I to other children we knew in means of gaining control. What hurt the most wasn't direct comparison, but a combination of praising other children, while withdrawing praise and affection from us, his own children. *Look at Angela, she is so gorgeous, like a real model! Adriana is such a great student. You are lucky to have such a daughter! That dress doesn't suit you. We better give it to Anna, she is much more developed than you are.* We felt like all other children are better students than us, all girls are prettier and more valuable than us, which is a very unhealthy mindset for a child to grow up with. We were at an imaginary competition with other children, and we felt like we were constantly losing. And while praising all other children in front of us, our success and talents were rarely to never highlighted in front of other people. This way, by using a comparison as his weapon, a narcissist keeps his children small, and ensures one thing he wants the most - the narcissistic supply. Because you are a "bad" child, you want to prove to yourself that you are as good as Adrianna, Anna or Angela, that you are worthy of praise and love, and you wanting to try harder to be a better daughter makes him feel like his opinion matters. You grow up feeling like you are not good enough, so your narcissistic father feels important and in control. Instead of teaching us how to love ourselves and see other children as our equals, all we saw is that they are great and we are not - other children are superior to us. After all, he imagined a much grander future for you, and you are not fulfilling it!

Acting flashy, overexaggerating and bragging about their child's endeavors is the flipside of the coin and another way a narcissistic father gains control. When a child starts to fulfill desires and ambitions of their father, excessive criticism quickly transforms into excessive praise and acknowledgment. Because a narcissistic father desires to be admired by others and in the center of attention, they use their child's success to put themselves in the spotlight and show the world how great of a job they did raising their child. However, they use this not only to get admiration, but to control the child and create memories a child can hold on to any time they start doubting their father's intentions, decisions or judgment. These moments create powerful positive memories, memories when a child feels important, seen, heard and acknowledged. This is how he gains his child's trust and ensures a solid narcissistic supply. These are the memories that keep you, as their child, hooked to them at your expense and keep you going back to their false safe shelter when you feel unsure of yourself. And they will do anything to make you feel insecure and vulnerable.

A narcissist uses these positive emotions and memories to make the child want to please and fulfill their father's narcissistic ideals and desires even more, which creates an endless spiral of feeling unworthy and wanting to prove one's worthiness to a narcissist. When I graduated, my father made a huge event to celebrate my graduation. When I got to a prestigious high school, something that he always wanted the two of us to do, he took us all on an exotic family trip. When my sister got her first and only modeling job, he gave her the permission to get a driver's license, something he would otherwise never do. These memories are rare, but they served our father for many years. Every time we confronted him about something, we'd feel guilty for doing so, even if we had a solid point and a complete right to voice our opinions. Memories like these were a vacuum that sucked us back in every time we tried to break the chain and become our own individuals and make our own decisions. We felt guilty for being disrespectful, when in reality, there was nothing disrespectful about choosing one's own path.

They control their children by being the ultimate provider, and this is a problem that usually erupts when a child tries to go off on their own, build an independent life, move and become an adult. This can be money, material wealth and support, but it can also be security or anything else they can provide, from something as big as a home to transportation. A narcissistic father feels threatened by these attempts and will sabotage them to ensure the child stays with them and validates their importance as a provider for as long as possible. *You won't be able to survive without my financial help; I am afraid it will be hard on you; being an adult is a lot of responsibility,* or *You don't even know how to cook and pay bills* are common comments a narcissist uses when trying to discourage attempts to leave the family nest, as if being an adult is not something that can be learned. They lure their children back in by letting them fail. The narcissist has taught his children that failure is equivalent to the end of the world, and not a chance to grow and learn; which is why many young adults go back to their families and their narcissistic fathers, discouraged from not being able to adapt to the new way of living, even though growing up is a complex process and we all fail until we learn. Because they don't have a healthy sense of self and are lacking in self-esteem, as narcissists purposely didn't help them prepare for the world of adults, and because many don't have a clear sense of identity, leaving the family home takes many attempts. They would withdraw all financial support if you decide to go and live on your own, but they will gladly finance you if you come back home. That is how the narcissist lures you back in and brings back control over their narcissistic supply - you. You depending on them makes them feel big and important. Remember, a narcissist does not want you to grow up, as that means you will no longer need them and will have nothing to owe them.

The interesting thing is, as much as they create these positive memories, they make them only when they feel like you are meeting their expectations. They will celebrate your achievements, flashily bragging about them only when they are part of their own vision, the vision of a perfect child. Even if I was never interested in medicine and am terrified of hospitals, on his demand, I did enroll to a prestigious medical school. Once I graduated, he threw a party equivalent to an engagement party. It was a huge deal to him. However, once he found out I enrolled in the University of Social Sciences to become a psychologist, he limited financial support, claiming I must take responsibility for my own choices. He never bragged about my success and was a great student. This kind of behavior, when the narcissist reinforces acts and decisions that fit into his criteria, and punishes and withdraws support when the child makes independent decisions, is called destructive conditioning. Narcissistic fathers make you feel guilty for pursuing your goals and dreams if these don't fit into their picture of how you are supposed to be. This includes them not paying attention to or not giving acknowledgments to your talents, and not praising your skills, even if you are exceptional.

You may be a fairly good artist who grew up thinking their art is average. Your father may discourage your attempts to join art clubs or competitions, deeming them a waste of time. You may show them your drawings and they would look at them with a blank expression as if they just looked at a tv show they aren't interested in. If they say your drawings are great, that "great" is not nearly as big as the one you'd get if you joined the volleyball team, something they thought you should do. Narcissistic fathers do this to shape your behavior and gain control over your life and how you spend your time. You drawing some foolish portraits won't make you a better volleyball player, so why waste your time on that? These may be small things, but for a child, their talents being ignored by someone who *knows better*, their father, is a real discouragement, to the point a child may even feel fearful of doing things they enjoy. Children are afraid of being judged, being seen as unsuccessful by their father. They want to avoid being yelled at, avoid criticism and they don't want to experience feeling unworthy, so they fall into the net of conditioning. Ultimately, a narcissistic father does not want you to do what makes you happy, but what makes them happy.

Chapter 6

Narcissistic fathers and unhealthy family dynamics

Since a narcissist sees themselves in light of grandiosity and the rest of the world needs to match the ideal image they have created in their head, family as the core base for raising a child becomes an unhealthy environment for a child to grow up in. The normal flow of affection and decision making is disrupted and the dynamic of the family becomes imbalanced - the father takes the center stage, the mother, a child, and their siblings second, third and fourth place. Narcissistic fathers see their family members as threats to their grandiosity, tools for making their value recognizable and making their ideals become a reality.

The narcissist needs to be the one everything in the family revolves around, from making tiny decisions to organizing and choosing a lifestyle of the entire family and each individual separately. They create a stage for them to be the main role by enabling their family members and creating a codependent environment. *Where would you be without me, If it wasn't for me you would be no one, If I didn't work so hard you'd be living on the streets now* and *You should be thankful for all I do for you* ...are some of the common phrases they use to make family members feel small and undervalued. The narcissistic father has a deep-rooted belief that everyone in the family should be thankful for having them in their lives, and everything that is done is done on their terms or not at all. There is a restriction of freedom and a need not to disturb the waters, rather than openly talk and share feelings, thoughts, and aspirations. The family itself, just like an individual relationship a narcissist has with each family member, is a roller coaster where children and the mother constantly experience highs and lows, frequently afraid of being themselves or doing something wrong - something that doesn't match the father's expectations.

Instead of collaboration, compromise, tolerance, and acceptance of one another, family members often feel as if they are in competition with one another, which is especially prominent in families when there are two or more children. In families when there is only one child, it is not uncommon to see a child and a mother being opposed to each other, all as a result of a narcissist trying to compare, blame and create a distance between them. Using previously described manipulation techniques, the narcissistic father sets the stage where family members are in competition to prove their worth to the narcissist, to prove they deserve love and to prove their value as human beings, as if they are not valuable without their father's affirmation. Love and support feel like limited sources and children frequently feel left out if their sibling gets more attention and affection from the narcissist. This can create envy, competitiveness, jealousy, hatred, feelings of rejection, unworthiness and abandonment in a child who is being ignored by a narcissist, and a sense of specialness, worthiness, success, recognition, and approval in a child who receives narcissistic love. This is until the tables turn when an adored child does something that is out of the balance with what the narcissistic father expects from them. Then, their roles reverse, which further amplifies competition between siblings and shifts the focus from the narcissist's maliciousness to family members themselves. The dislike, jealousy, and anger is not directed towards the father but towards the other sibling, who stole the spotlight from them, so they need to work hard to win back the father's love. Narcissists classify their children as good or bad compared to how well they fit into their image of a perfect child. It is very common for one child to become the perfect, favorite "golden" child, and the other a scapegoat, a bad child, and a constant disappointment for the family.

The treatment a child gets from the narcissist and the place it earns in a narcissist's life depends on various things: how the child fits into the father's ideal, how good of a narcissistic supply it provides and how successful it is in pleasing the father compared to other children and the mother. The family has a hierarchy, where the narcissistic father always needs to be on top, and all other members rank depending on how well they fit into what the narcissist finds acceptable and how much of an ego boost they give him. There is no sense of unity as the core of the family is based on competition, manipulation, and fear.

The mother of a child, another important figure that should enjoy equality when it comes to raising a child, is frequently portrayed by the father as an enemy. *She is the one to be blamed for your failures, she is the one responsible for all the bad things happening in the family, she is the sabotager and the bad guy. It is all your mother's fault. She raised you to be lazy.* Her words and promises are usually made irrelevant, even if what she's doing is truly better for the child. This is the constant scapegoat and an example of how a child should not be, as the narcissist is always in competition for attention and the child's mother is his greatest competitor. Many times, these women suffered narcissistic abuse themselves, they are devalued and as a result they find it difficult to trust themselves and make independent decisions. Their lives, like their children's lives are micromanaged by the main star in the family, who always knows best - the narcissistic father. The mother is frequently hushed and taught to follow her husband's authority. She is expected to be, and frequently is, submissive, having very little power over what a narcissist does and decisions he makes for the family.

Narcissists establish their manipulation and control through relatives, grandparents, neighbors and family friends as well, by making them their advocates. A flying monkey is every individual, part of the family or not, that contributes, consciously or not, to narcissistic manipulation of a father by supporting their actions and ways of raising children. These people act on behalf of the narcissist by reinforcing their statements and behaviors. They are the ones to say things such as - *You are lucky to have such a father; You should be thankful for how tolerant your father is of your behavior; Your father did everything for you and this is how you repay him; He is doing this for your best interest; Your father knows what is right for you.* Many times, people who play the role of the flying monkey truly believe the father is doing what's best for their child and there are cases when they don't have malicious intentions and are, just like family members themselves, manipulated by the narcissist and seduced by their charm.

This is how paternal narcissism takes a toll on children on a much larger scale. Narcissistic fathers don't only affect their children directly, but they affect the whole environment in which the child grows up.

Chapter 7

The scapegoat vs. the golden child

I mentioned in the previous chapter how competitive the nature of family dynamics get when your father is a narcissist. If you are their child, you could be one of two things. You are either adored, praised and worshiped or you are blamed for everything, criticized and ignored. In other words, you are the golden child or the scapegoat. These two epithets are what shaped your mentality long before you could wrap your head around how negative of an impact your father has on your mental health. Being one or the other is nothing you can choose or change. These roles are given to you and your siblings without your consent or contribution.

Narcissistic fathers don't see their children as individuals whose authenticity he needs to cherish, but he sees them as either acceptable and a boost to their ego or the complete opposite, the disturber of their imaginary authority. Being who you essentially are, your nature as a child, and your characteristics, are what poses you to take on one of these two roles, in the narcissist's eyes. Narcissistic fathers carefully analyze and examine their children at a very young age. A child's temperament, intellect, character, behavior, curiosity or lack of it, calmness or liveliness are all contributing factors to the roles they will have growing up. It is nothing you chose to be. It is who your father chose you to be. Being a child of a narcissist, I always felt like an outcast in the family. While our father's narcissism affected us differently, both me and my sister needed to re-parent ourselves as adults as we both struggled with low self-esteem, self-doubt, serious fears of abandonment and depression. I was the rebel, and she was the calm one. She was the golden child and I was the scapegoat. And because you don't get to choose those roles, you easily become your father's puppet and play that role without knowing how or why you got it. Not only do you play the given role, but you also know very well what role other family members play and so you play along. So, if your sibling was the golden child, you will grow up thinking they are special and every other family member will treat them as such. And if you are a scapegoat like I was, every family member and many people who are close to your family members will see you as the peace disturber. It follows you everywhere and affects all areas of your life, not only what you live through being part of such a dysfunctional family. Both the scapegoat and the golden child are imaginary identities, not something the child actually is.

The terms scapegoat and golden child are prominent in psychological practice and are often used to label individuals who are dealing with people who are targets of various psychopathic, sociopathic, malignant and narcissistic personalities. The scapegoat is a person who is constantly blamed or criticized for wrongdoings of others. They are obligated to take on responsibilities both for their doings, and the doings of others, taking on burdens they don't have to carry. The scapegoat is the black sheep of the family. A child who gets to play this role is usually labeled as the bad child, the one who behaves badly, who is not as good as their sister or brother, the one who always makes mistakes. You are chosen to be the scapegoat not because you are bad or less loveable, but because you are seen as a threat, a wild child, the one who needs to be tamed, a threat to your father's sense of control and unfortunately, this is what you don't understand when you are a child. If you were the scapegoat, everything bad that happens in the family is your fault, no matter if it's something you actually did or not, and no matter your actual contribution to the unfortunate situation you are blamed for.

Since I was the scapegoat of my family, I was the one who is responsible for everything and everyone. I was expected to excel at things, be responsible, be mature before I needed to be, do things for family members and take care of them, but never appreciated for the things I did. If my sister did something that disturbed the calm waters, I was the one expected to correct that. Matter of fact, I was not only expected to make things right, but I was blamed for giving bad examples, making her do something against her will, and not affecting her decisions. If she got into trouble it was because of me. If a fight would happen, it was because of me. If someone got yelled at and screamed at, it was me. I was the child who would get all the rage from her parents simply because they had a bad day at work, the one to be blamed because the house is not clean, as if I was the only one who needs to take care of the home when the mother is away. Responsibilities were never shared, and while my sister was only expected to have good grades, I needed to do the same, along with taking care of the home, doing chores, taking care of our animals, and going shopping. If I asked for the chores to be shared, I was blamed for sabotaging her, as she had better things to do and work on her talents. That was never enough, and it was never appreciated or praised.

Golden children, on the other hand, live to tell different stories about their childhood. The golden child or the perfect child, although raised in the same family is the one who gets the opposite treatment. They are praised for everything they do, they are idealized, and put on a pedestal. They are the narcissistic father's favorite child. They are the ones showered with affection, attention, love and gifts. The golden child is the one who does everything right, who is talented, gifted and worthy of praise. In other words, they are the polar opposites of the scapegoat. However, just like the role of a scapegoat, the role of a golden child is as equally imposed and something the child did not choose to be. The narcissist chose them. Contrary to the scapegoat who is opinionated, who is considered to be the opposer, the golden child is usually the one who follows the rules and doesn't make much fuss about what their narcissistic father expects them to do. Furthermore, they are reinforced to follow the narcissist and give them unlimited narcissistic supply, because the narcissist praises them, supports them and idealizes what they do. As a result, such children grow up feeling they deserve special treatment wherever they go, they think they are somehow special, unique and better than others.

Siblings who grew up with narcissistic fathers frequently have completely different perceptions of each other, their father and their childhood. While one would say they felt invisible and sad, unappreciated, the other would say they had the perfect childhood, that they were loved and cared for. This is how great of a difference a narcissistic father can make and how drastically different experiences their children have based on narcissistic favoritism. Unfortunately, this difference in treatment not only affects how children see themselves, but it also affects their relationship, which becomes highly competitive and toxic from a very young age. Siblings don't see each other as support but as a threat and rivals. They are opposed to each other and in a constant fight for their father's approval. All children are unfortunately part of the endless race for approval and love from their father. Many times, a child who is the scapegoat has many talents, but isn't appreciated for them because it doesn't go well with their role of being the one who makes mistakes all the time. Conversely, the golden child may not be as talented, by they can be praised and worshiped for the talents they do have or things they are average at only because they are the golden child.

The roles children play are based on how obedient they are or not. While the scapegoat usually has stronger will and is willing to speak up, in the narcissist's mind that needs to be suppressed so the scapegoat is more obedient and willing to cater to their father's wishes. Children are in constant opposition, may grow up trying to sabotage each other, put each other down and frequently grow apart, having a very disconnected and distant relationship. The relationship of the scapegoat and the golden child is not based on mutual trust, respect and sibling love, but on animosity, hatred, jealousy, and distrust. By putting children against each other, a narcissistic father ensures narcissistic supply from all of his children. The scapegoats feed his ego by trying to prove themselves worthy and trying harder to be responsible and mature, and the golden child feeds their ego by being like them, following rules, adoring the narcissist, never questioning their authority and ultimately, wanting to be like the narcissist. Siblings fighting among each other for their father's approval make him feel special and important, which is extremely destructive for the whole family.

This war for approval, the war between the golden child who wants to be even more adored, and the one who fights hard for crumbs of attention, continues even in adulthood. Unfortunately, both roles have their pitfalls and neither the scapegoat nor the golden child leave that war unbruised. The identities that were given to them are false and it is a matter of time, usually in early adulthood, when these false identities start creating troubles in both the scapegoat's and golden child's life. And although opposed their whole lives, none of them actually gets to the top. The narcissistic treatment leaves marks on one's personality and requires a lot of reality-checks, self-awareness and re-parenting, which many children can't cope with. For the golden child, adulthood becomes a dangerous territory they are afraid to enter, and so many of them mature much later than their peers, staying close to their narcissistic father and the false sense of security he has created. Although not a general rule, it is not uncommon for these children to develop narcissistic traits themselves, as they spend so much time trying to be like the father. They are usually less mature, their emotions are infantile and their reactions to not getting what they want are similar to their fathers reactions. In this war, the golden child may even try to sabotage the scapegoat, lie about them, put them down, make them take on the blame for something they did and get away with things easily, something their sibling never gets to do just for the fact that they are the family's scapegoat. It is not uncommon for scapegoats and golden children to live completely different lives, behave completely different and have completely different perceptions of their own family and its members, even though they were raised under the same roof, all due to separation made by their father. A child of a narcissist is either constantly praised or criticized and not good enough, and when these two polar opposites are split between two or more children, his children get triggered into disliking their own brother or sister.

If you have a narcissistic father and this sounds familiar, the sad, painful truth is, it is not anyone's fault. Neither of you chose to be one or the other. You are both victims of an enlarged, hungry for attention ego that got the chance to be attached to the role of a father. The narcissist is to be blamed for the animosity created between you and your siblings, but growing up, it will never seem like it is their fault, because such a father is so busy creating the scenarios where you and your siblings need to fight for his attention and validation. Narcissistic fathers are extremely good at it.

Because they are taught that they are special, golden children are less likely to take on the path of healing, although they need it as much as the scapegoat does. This is because they like to believe what they were told they are their whole life, while the scapegoat is left drowning in self-doubt from day one and as they grow up, they are more likely to want to strengthen and learn to value themselves. Unfortunately, as much as being adored by their narcissistic father makes their life seemingly easier, it can be a great obstacle later in life, when they face the reality, and that is that the outer world does not recognize their talents as much their father did and it is usually in adulthood when golden children of a narcissist find it very difficult to deal with reality, having to be treated as ordinary. Do know that roles can be reversed as the father finds it suitable. The golden child does get criticized and love is withdrawn from them when and if they try to rebel. The scapegoat gets their bits and pieces of admiration when they follow their fathers ideal, but these moments are usually short-lived. The reversal of roles serves to reinforce the narcissistic supply. If you are a single child, it is possible that you took on both of these roles, depending on your behavior.

What is important to know is that neither of them is initially good or bad, less or more loveable. They are just as equally victims of narcissism, although it may take a different toll on them. No matter which role you played, one of the next chapters will be dedicated to healing that is available to all children who suffered the effects of paternal narcissism, as all of them need to rediscover themselves, find their identity and learn what it means to truly love themselves, without the need to be externally validated.

Chapter 8

The wounds of the scapegoated child

Being a scapegoat in my family and the ultimate black sheep, I know first-hand how it feels to be rejected by your own family. A sense of belonging, safety, and unconditional love are something I didn't receive. Growing up, I remember feeling like life is unjust most of the time. No matter what you do, no matter how hard you try, your efforts are somehow never good enough. If you do something great, win a contest or get a good grade, you might get a short bravo from your father, but shortly after, everyone in the family forgets about your great achievement and you get back to being the scapegoat, who never does anything right. There you are, giving your maximum effort to be seen and loved, only to get crumbs of affection. This is the pattern that I unconsciously accepted later on, which furthermore sealed my destiny and prevented me from gaining the success I now know I deserve. just like everyone else. It always confused me how people outside our family would perceive my father as the amazing dad and my family the ideal family, when I was living in that home, feeling sad, invisible and anxious every day of my life. I thought, well it must be that I am imagining things, it must be that I am really bad. I was the one who overreacts, who is overly sensitive and who imagines things. Little did I know.

If you are the scapegoat, you are constantly hushed, your sense of fashion is unacceptable, you are antisocial, the weird one, the bad student, the clumsy, the stupid, you name it. You are the one who carries the blame on your shoulder for the things you did not do and things you shouldn't be responsible for. You are responsible for your brother or sister, for family pets and their wellbeing, for hygiene at home, for your father's health. Whatever crisis your family went through, you were probably in the middle of the battlefield, the one to be blamed. You are never good enough, the one who deeply believes that you need to be perfect or you will never be loved. The one that needs to stay silent and tone down the voice if something feels unfair, the one who has no right to voice your opinion. And growing up, you probably wanted to fight for your equality, even as a child, by voicing how you feel, only to be put down and criticized for it.

Scapegoats feel unloved, unseen, unappreciated and unheard very early on in their childhood. They grow up thinking they are somehow not important, and not understanding why. Deprived of attention and loving from their father, invisible to the entire family, and conditioned to believe that they are somehow inherently bad or not good enough, these children grow up to have very low self-esteem, distorted images of oneself and lack of belief in one's talents and abilities. Children of narcissistic fathers are never loved for who they are, but for how well they cater to him, and in case the of the scapegoated child, their father's conditional love reaches extremes and creates a negative self-image, destroys and diminishes the child's self-respect and self-love. Matter of fact, scapegoats find it very difficult to love themselves later in life, no matter how much they have achieved or how hard they have worked. Just like the golden child who thinks everyone should cater to them, the scapegoat feels like no matter how much they improve themselves, they are always one step behind everyone else. They don't recognize their talents and skills, as they were discouraged to pursue their passions or their talents were never given attention. This twisted perception of themselves is linked to poor self-image, lack of assertiveness, anxiety, fear of being judged and rejected, which is how they were raised to be. Many of us scapegoats suffered from depression, as we were made to believe that we are simply not loveable for who we are. This translates into all interpersonal relationships we have later in life. The inability to set and voice one's boundaries and the learned role of the scapegoat, unfortunately, bring more people who treat us just like our father did. Many of the relationships scapegoats have are a projection of their relationships with the father, and so, unfortunately, it is not uncommon for them to end up in toxic, abusive relationships, with emotionally unavailable people who see them as their narcissistic father does - as scapegoats. This way, the effects of paternal narcissism take a much larger scale and learned behavior transpired in all other areas of a scapegoat's life until they become ready to re-parent themselves.

Because you have your own inner guidance that

something is wrong or right, every time you felt like voicing it and standing up for yourself as a child you would be punished and made very guilty. The scapegoat is the child who feels the rage of their father while watching him treat other siblings with kindness and love. They are the ones who are ashamed of themselves, disappointed in themselves and those children who feel lonely in their own homes. If your sibling did something wrong, you were probably the one to be blamed for it. A narcissistic father uses guilt traps, gaslighting, offensive comments, and blame games to make you stay silent and stop threatening their sense of grandiosity. This is the child who receives the silent treatment the most of all family members. If you needed something from your father, you probably had to work for it twice as hard to prove yourself to them. The scapegoat, because they have more trouble following rules, are the ones who need to fulfill more terms and conditions than other children. Narcissistic fathers constantly compare the scapegoat to other children, and in that comparison, put their own child on the lowest levels of comparison charts. *Why can't you be more like your sister or brother* is a common comparison and can be very hurtful, as the child is made to feel like they are less than, the less important child and the less valuable one.

The dynamic of the relationship between the narcissistic father and the scapegoat is rooted in the narcissist's shadow side, his deepest fears and insecurities. He not only sees this child as a threat to his imaginary authority and sense of grandiosity, but he also sees and projects his own fears onto the child. The scapegoated child is the embodiment of his fears and as such, it needs to be punished, criticized and rejected. The scapegoate child may be very talented and have a great potential for success, much greater than the golden child, but in the narcissists' mind, this potential needs to be tamed and kept under control, as no one else gets to be the star but himself. This is why the child who is like him and worships him, is the perfect child who gets to be worshiped, as that child is more likely to be his follower and never take on the lead role. Children of narcissistic fathers are either a projection of his wishes and dreams, in which the child worships him and fulfills his ambitions, or his fears, where the child stands up for itself, confronts him or gets to have the center stage. The scapegoat feels unloved and will do anything to gain their father's appreciation and love, especially at a young age, and so they will put more effort into being more worthy of their father's affection. This feeds the father's ego and acts and becomes counterproductive for the child, because the narcissist feels important when their child fights so hard to win their affection, and so they will withdraw their praise even more, making the scapegoat feel even more unworthy.

One of the hardest things for a child to understand is why are they so marginalized and why they don't receive love from their father. It is hard to find reasoning why, despite all the effort to be better, work harder and be responsible, even when some responsibilities are not your burden to bear, you feel unloved and abandoned by your father. What you need to know is that you were chosen to be the scapegoat for a reason, but that reason is not what you thought. You were chosen because as a child you had an independent spirit, which posed a threat to your narcissistic father. The scapegoat is not the child who is bad, less talented or unlovable, but a child who has strong willpower, a child who questions and resists authority and a child who, from a very young age, has a strong inner compass for what is right and wrong. Children who are chosen for this role also have a higher inclination to be highly empathetic, and therefore easier to manipulate through blaming and guilt, as they are more likely to internalize blame. These children are less willing to obey, especially if they find something is unjust, and these traits defy the narcissist and his manipulation attempts. Because of these traits, the scapegoat won't cater to their father and enable them with the constant narcissistic supply by giving constant admiration, so they will be dismissed, discarded, criticized and put down for opposing the narcissist.

A narcissistic father programs all his children to cater to him one way or the other. The narcissistic father wants you to be below them. They don't want you to grow up to be a strong, independent individual who speaks their truth. Narcissists are predatory people and every relationship they have, including relationships with their children, is a constant battle for power where they have to be the winner. Your virtues are turned against you, solely for the purpose of your father having to prove to himself how grandiose and important he is. The programming of the scapegoated child is such that their justice-seeking, caring and empathetic nature is not nourished, but used against them. They grow up catering to other people's needs and in this way, the father's programming finds a way to intoxicate all the future relationships. They are programmed to take care of other people and believe it is their responsibility to enable other people, take care of their emotional wellbeing and take all the responsibility for the success of the relationship onto themselves. If a scapegoat fails to do so, and tries to put themselves, their needs and wants before others, they will feel an immense amount of guilt and shame. They will live their lives trying to please other people only to escape feeling these negative emotions because they are taught that caring for oneself is selfish. Until we start healing, we end up in toxic, one-sided and abusive relationships with selfish individuals, narcissists, psychopaths, emotionally unavailable and manipulative people, because of this false belief that we are to blame if something goes wrong. We need to prove to someone that we are lovable by taking care of their needs and fixing relationships. We become a magnet for people who treat us like our father did because we don't know that love and genuine relationships feel good and replenish our spirit. We don't know what true love is because, in our subconscious mind, we need to earn it, and to earn it we need to put everyone else before us. Relationships end up draining us and only rarely nourishing us back.

Most of these children are forced to grow up faster because of all the responsibility and guilt that has been placed upon them. They believe being spontaneous or failing at something is a disaster that only proves how unworthy they are because that is how they were raised.

When they grow up, scapegoats take criticism to heart and take rejection much more personally, for which they are sometimes deemed by their peers as being too sensitive. Paternal narcissism is an invisible threat to a child's integrity and identity, which shows in adulthood, and because it is so hard to pinpoint what exactly is wrong in one's upbringing, scapegoats rarely find understanding and compassion from people around them.

If you are a scapegoat, because you so deeply believe that to be loved you need to be perfect, more successful or better looking , you may find it hard to enjoy life the way others do. You are taught to believe that only perfection is worthy of admiration and that you can't be loved just for being who you are. Scapegoats grow up learning to accept the blame and guilt that was never theirs to begin with, but they also frequently become overachievers, where they are constantly hunting for the next big thing that will help them prove to their fathers that they were wrong, which they don't know is impossible to achieve. And while they are constant overachievers, no matter how successful they become, scapegoats always feel like something is missing, like that success is somehow not enough, finding it hard to praise themselves for all the hard work they have done. Many of us develop perfectionism that is mostly directed inwards. Many take on more than they can carry, take responsibilities for other people, solving their problems and being scapegoats for everyone, which is one of the ways narcissistic fathers deem their scapegoated children to failure. These children don't put themselves first and they believe acknowledging their needs and wants is selfish, feeling guilty and ashamed in moments when they do try to take care of themselves because that is what their father taught them. In adulthood, when the scapegoat manages to live independently, until the healing process takes place and they learn to reestablish themselves, many associate themselves with friends or partners who, just like their father, demand to take the center stage, dominate and take emotional or other resources from the scapegoat. What you've learned by being the scapegoated child is hard to shake off. The combination of pressure to succeed and prove one's worth, while feeling unlovable, rejecting one's needs and taking on too many responsibilities ultimately leads not only to low self-esteem, but to depression and anxiety. The toll paternal narcissism takes on a child is huge, and goes way beyond what you experience in the family. Depression, suicidal thoughts, loss of faith in the world around you and yourself, loss of trust and hope and failed attempts to rebuild oneself are just some of these devastating effects. Scapegoated children find it difficult to heal, because they see setbacks in the healing process as failures, as they are hard on themselves due to the difficult upbringing they had.

Ultimately, as a scapegoat, you feel like you don't matter. Like you are not important. You are invisible and feel like a failure, despite all the success you have achieved. As you grow old, you learn that being raised by a narcissistic father and being a scapegoat for many other people in your life, that the only person you can rely on is yourself. But you also learn that the only person you have is you, which is one of the first steps to healing. One day, you wake up and feel like you don't want to let yourself down, and that you don't want to let a narcissist shape your life anymore. And one day you decide to give yourself the love you always deserved, without waiting on your father to tell you how great you are, and how after all, you are a child worthy of love and admiration. You stop wanting to make your family proud, but instead shift your focus on being gentle with yourself and being proud of how far you've come. Because you have, and you deserve to be happy.

Chapter 9

Narcissistic fathers, their sons, and daughters

There is an unwritten rule in society that having a father, no matter how emotionally and mentally healthy or capable of raising a child he is, is better than having no father figure at all. Fathers are harshly judged only in cases of complete abandonment and physical violence, and so narcissistic abuse is usually off the radar. Narcissistic fathers do not differentiate their children only based on how threatened they are by a child's qualities or how well the child fits into their idealized image. Besides setting up their children for scapegoat or golden child programming, they treat their boys and girls differently. Because a narcissist wants to be recognized in society, they want their child to succeed and right the wrongs, proving the world how truly amazing they are, by living through their children. Since narcissistic fathers can't build love-based relationships, this inability creates a dysfunctional dynamic in how they relate to children of both sexes. Because their children are an extension of themselves, the narcissist sees and treats them as belongings rather than children with their own needs, thoughts, and emotions. Although children of both sex can be scapegoated or seen as perfect children and both suffer from the same psychological and emotional consequences, the narcissistic father relates differently to their sons and daughters, and the following text will give insight as to how.

Narcissistic father-daughter relationships

We have mentioned the malicious nature of their personality and their predatory approach, where they use a child's weakness against them. In society, fathers are seen as protectors, providers, mature, wise and stable, and this is something the narcissist knows how to use to their advantage. Their girls are not only seen as property but because of the societal image of what the role of a father is, they are, in their father's eyes, easier to manipulate under the parole: *I just want to keep you safe from the harsh, cruel world that can only harm you.* The world is a dangerous place, so these girls need to stay protected and safe from harm where, in reality, the real danger is the manipulator who raises them. The narcissist is a master of disguise, and frequently, everyone who is not a family member will see them as caring fathers who try their best to make a stable foundation for their daughters - they are their rock and greatest support. As a result, their daughters are overprotected, grow up to be fearful and anxious about asserting themselves, frequently feeling unworthy of love, success or happiness.

Such a father doesn't want their daughters to grow up or become independent as that means losing narcissistic supply. They will do anything to keep you small and make you believe you can't take care of yourself, so naturally, every attempt to be your own person and grow up will be discouraged and sabotaged. Nothing matters more than staying in control and nothing matters less than how you feel and what path you'd like to follow. One survivor I talked to had a father who would constantly criticize her for spending money and not becoming independent like all her peers. And yet, every time she attempted to break free and become independent, her father would say she is not capable enough, mature enough and that she won't be able to do it on her own without family financial support. This mind game not only diminishes all efforts of authenticity, but it also ensures a stable narcissistic supply - *You depend on me, so I will make sure you feel bad about it, and yet I will sabotage every effort you make in trying to be self-reliant.* A narcissist, just like in all other areas of life, has an idealized image of how they want to be treated, and in a family environment this means they want to be the ones everyone worships, listens to and respects.

They want a perfect family they think they deserve, where their daughters fit the image of daughters from Hollywood movies, who are sweet, humble, nicely dressed, don't rebel against norms or their father's expectations. If your father wanted you to be a feminine, nice behaving lady, and you happened to be the artistic type with your own fashion sense, they probably would make sure you feel horrible about the way you look. Narcissistic fathers keep their daughters small, by putting them down, discouraging them and dismissing anything that deviates from their own perception of how a daughter *should be*. Anything that represents an expression of individuality, be it physical looks, personal beliefs, opinions, interests, ambitions, emotions or goals, is seen as unwanted, unacceptable and disrespectful. Choices are not allowed. Any form of normal, healthy desire to express oneself causes the narcissistic father to act passive-aggressive, to rage, ignore, dismiss or punish you.

Dating and socializing is another area of scrutiny, as every person who threatens to take away their narcissistic supply is perceived as a threat and needs to be eliminated. Such fathers either criticize any relationships their daughters have or act uninterested in their social life until the daughter does something that defies the narcissist's code of behavior, which is when the punishment takes the form of forbidding or sabotaging their daughters right to socialize or date. Choosing a group of friends, dating, let alone moving out and living with your partner, are out of the question. Additionally, narcissistic fathers may raise their daughters to distrust men in general. Every man, except their father, is a threat, wants to use them, abuse them and take something away, and while daughters of narcissistic fathers may grow up thinking that men are not to be trusted, they are raised by a real abuser. Frequently, she may even end up with narcissistic, toxic and abusive men which makes her father's prophecy come true. What these women fail to realize, until later in life during their healing journey, is that these are patterns their father taught them and so they seek the same kind abusers their father was, not knowing the real root of toxic relationships they engage themselves in.

Many daughters grow up thinking their fathers wanted to protect them and keep them safe, where in reality, what they discover as they grow up is that the only thing their fathers wanted is to feel important, in control and validated themselves. They wanted a pat on the shoulder from others for how good of a job they did raising their girls, and they wanted to be perceived as the authority they believed they are. These daughters are more often than not prone to harsh self-criticism, self-sabotaging and self-blaming behaviors later in life. One daughter of a narcissistic father I had a chance to meet struggled with anorexia and depression, as her father pushed her to be a model from the age of thirteen. She wasn't allowed to play volleyball as that wasn't very feminine and won't flatter her body, which is one of many examples that speaks to how toxic and destructive being raised by someone who has NPD really is. That is something we will dive more into in the chapter that follows.

Narcissistic father-son relationship

While their little girls are manipulated under the narcissist's parole *I am your protector, I will keep you safe from harm*, their boys are raised in a different manner. Projection, in the case of father-son relationships, becomes even more visible, as the son is not only the person who can make his father look great, but he is also the object onto which the narcissistic father rejects his masculinity and every masculine trait he sees in himself. His desire to dominate, win, gain power, success, and recognition get a more aggressive expression in relation to his son.

Because, in his mind, a narcissistic father's genius and talent are not recognized, he wants his son to prove to the outer world that he, his blood, is the powerful genius he believes himself to be. In other words, he projects his grandiosity and lives through his son, wanting his own child to be a living example of his narcissistic grandiose ideals. He does this by *teaching him how to be a real man,* glorifying overly assertive and pushy behavior, ruthless dominance, rage, anger and other unacceptable ways of acting and relating to others. He encourages his son to push the limits, regardless of how the child feels about it, even inappropriately aggressive and confrontational behavior beyond the child's natural comfort zone and regardless of their temperament. This is a projection, as supporting such behavior reflects the way he himself protects his imaginary authority - through placing his authority upon others and gaining control over them. However, promoting and advocating for behavior does not rely on encouragement, real support and healthy building of the child's self-esteem through collaboration, but on negative emotions and reactions such as fear, anger, rage, guilt, anxiety, stress or blame. He teaches his daughters that he, their narcissistic father, is the ultimate provider and the safe harbor they can trust. He does the same with his sons, but in a slightly different way. He teaches his daughter to fear the exterior world, and their son to hate and feel threatened by the outer world, which is exactly the mixture of emotions he, himself, feels. He portrays other people as a vile competition, an endless tournament where there can be only one winner, which is his son.

Being emotionally distant and unable to empathize, he tries to program his son to discard his own emotions and be ashamed of them, regardless of the child's true affectionate nature. Emotions need to be ignored, suppressed and stand in contrast to masculine roles the narcissist wants their son to take on. Even though the father may have a seemingly emotional bond with his son, this bond usually revolves around negative feelings and represents, just like with other family members, a roller coaster of shame, guilt, and anger versus adoration, glorification, and idealization. A child's true emotions, unless they are a reflection of how the father feels, are dismissed, ignored and if confessed, usually criticized, made fun of or made irrelevant. Ultimately, he wants his son to claim the dominance and recognition in the world he did not succeed in getting – he lives through his son, at his own child's expense. Just like with his daughter, his son's natural talents, temperament, affectionate nature, thoughts and character are not taken into account, and can frequently be harshly criticized. Behind the mask of a father who wants the best for his son - the best career, status recognition, the idea of ideal love - lies a selfish man, who wants to see part of him be revived and get a second chance to earn the alpha male recognition through his son. In relation to women, he may teach his son to disrespect, distrust, take what he needs from them, seduce and use them by telling tales of bad examples and experiences he has had or covertly, by putting his wife down or blaming her for all the upheaval the family has experienced. In his own mind, he is usually the great seducer and charmer and that is what he wants his son to become, as he is his living legacy and an object he lives through and a chance to redeem himself. When the son fails to fulfill his expectations, however, his narcissistic father gets enraged, dismisses, punishes and ignores the child as he himself is living through his son's failure or rejection. *You are weak. You will never become a man. You are a failure. No one will ever respect you. You are a disappointment. You let them win. You let them humiliate you. You are a coward. You let them take the prize.* Instead of offering his child support during challenging times, which he is unable to do, he amplifies the failure as he feels it himself. It is never about his son, but it is about him, as deep down, he has experienced rejection, humiliation or failure and this seriously threatens his enlarged ego and doesn't sit well with his agenda. As a result, the son feels an immense amount of shame, embarrassment, and guilt, and will, as a result, try hard not to disappoint his father again, and by doing so he is giving the father the ultimate narcissistic supply.

Chapter 10

The effects of paternal narcissism on children

Unfortunately, the devastating effect of paternal narcissism doesn't stop in family, but it expands into adulthood, whether or not there is direct contact with the father. Narcissistic fathers leave a big mark on their children, and so each aspect of their lives mirrors and repeats this unhealthy father-child relationship and learned patterns to an extent. Children who have such a parent can sense the effects of toxic paternal relationships in their friendships, love life, career and life choices. Such upbringing leaves an imprint on one's psyche in a few ways I will talk about below.

Before you start reading, just know this - Your childhood wasn't your choice and the life you are living now is a reflection of the many years of limitation, negative conditioning and mistreatment you have received. If the content below becomes triggering, remember that it is ok to feel the way you feel and to feel triggered. Know that I have felt the same way and that there are other fellow survivors who understand you on a deep level. You may feel like an injustice has been done to you, you may feel life is unfair because you didn't get to choose a better life for yourself when you were younger. You may feel anger or sadness.

Whatever you feel, you allow yourself to embrace the feeling. These are natural responses so be gentle with yourself. That is part of your journey and there is nothing shameful or weak about you if you have experienced or are experiencing any of the following effects of being raised by a narcissistic father. Take a deep breath, here we go.

Engaging in unhealthy relationships

Do you feel like your friends and partners are using you?

Do you feel emotionally drained by most people you closely relate to?

Do they make you feel guilty or bad about yourself?

Do you feel like your partners and friends don't care much about you?

Do you feel unloved and unappreciated by them?

If you have found yourself surrounded by friends or partners who used you, were selfish, deceitful or manipulative and you are a child of a narcissistic father, it might comfort you to know that your choice of partners or friends wasn't your fault. Your choice of people is part of your programming and a continuation of the role your father gave you. Here is how.

Children of narcissistic fathers attach their ability to

give and receive love to their ability to provide for others, many times not getting the same in return from their partners. Narcissistic fathers make their children feel like whatever they do isn't enough, and so once they reach adulthood, they will stretch themselves too thin in order to maintain toxic, one-sided relationships and friendships. They will crave love the same way they craved it from their father, where nothing was ever enough and they were taken advantage of or unappreciated.

They surround themselves with energy vampires who will always make them feel like what they are giving is not enough They are prone to be gaslighted, frequently in a position where they are taken advantage of, used, abused, manipulated or lied to, because that is the shadow they have been living under their whole life. One feels drawn, repelled and obligated to engage in activities and relationships that don't favor them at the same time and many close interactions reflect the father-child relationship, on more or less conscious levels. Relationships feel like a prison that is hard to escape, yet the prison one continuously puts themselves in is due to the inability to receive love as they were never taught how to. At the end of each relationship, one feels unheard, mistreated, used and abandoned, just like they felt in the family.

Through shame and guilt, two major tools used for programming a child's behavioral responses, the narcissist also creates the predisposition for failed or abusive relationships their children have. These children, including myself, before the healing occurs can find it extremely hard to say no to people. This inability to say no to other people's demands is extremely draining and can create the perfect base for anxiety, frustration, and depression. Because we were taught that living for ourselves and acknowledging our needs is selfish and bad, and because love is conditional and needs to be earned, we would often go out of our way to please other people and put their needs before our own. Furthermore, it may even be difficult to identify, understand and accept our needs, as it is not uncommon to immerse ourselves into other people and merge identities with them, just as we did with our father. This subconscious mechanism drives us to believe that doing things for others, doing favors, salvaging relationships and fighting for them, will bring us love and recognition because we don't know any better. Our worth depends on how well we manage to satisfy other people's demands and respond to their needs, and we may even seek out people who are very dramatic, attention-seeking and demanding as a result of that subconscious need. This way, narcissistic fathers extend their toxicity which continues to take a toll on our mental health. In other words, it is guilt, rather than love that drives most of our relationships until we recognize that we are repeating lessons our father taught us.

Children of narcissistic parents have a belief that if they worked harder at bettering themselves, if they had been a better partner or a friend, and accommodated other people's needs more, they would get a different outcome other than failed relationships. They genuinely think other people's problems are their responsibilities and all upheavals their fault and their burden to carry, while feeling unloved, uncared for and unappreciated by the same people they put before themselves.

While they take on responsibility for every failure in their personal life, they also take the blame that comes with it, and take downfalls as proof that they didn't give their best. They think they always could have done more, while ironically giving their last atoms of strength to cater to other people's needs. Because they were not valued and they spent their whole childhood enabling and providing narcissistic supply, they don't feel valuable unless they are in the role of a caretaker, frequently seeking romantic partners that are unavailable, need help, salvation or to be fixed. More so, they have the compulsion to fix and take responsibility for other people's actions, as they truly believe it is their fault if the relationship goes wrong.

The place in other people's lives is not given freely, but needs to be earned by investing and trying hard to make it work, even if the other party isn't giving back the same effort, or is even abusing this caretaker quality. One's value is directly linked to their ability to fix and change someone or win their love by trying hard and going above and beyond for them. In reality, people they engage with are hardly ever changing and the child of a narcissist will see rejection and failure as their own fault and the proof that they, after all, are not loveable.

Mental health problems

Are you struggling with depression?

Do you feel anxious and paralyzed with fear without knowing why?

Do you find it hard to participate in your own life?

Does your mood change unexpectedly and without warning?

Do you feel distant from yourself or feeling emotionally numb?

The hardest to deal with and the most dangerous effects paternal narcissism leaves on children is depression, eating disorders, anxiety, panic attacks, and different phobias. While depression and other mental health problems can happen to anyone, being raised by a narcissistic father can create a much more solid foundation for mental health issues to occur. Children of narcissistic fathers frequently battle with mental health issues and may display avoidant behaviors and phobias connected to the way they relate to people and their immediate environment. Constant uncertainty, emotional detachment and gaslighting, followed by a clouded identity, create space for the mind of the child to turn to defense mechanisms and behavior patterns.

Because the emotional self was restricted and emotions weren't heard or allowed to be expressed, a child of a narcissistic father may develop different affective disorders. We are taught that emotions mean weakness, they are unjustified and unacceptable and so we spend a lot of mental energy trying to be strong when we are not, which ultimately leads to trouble with intimacy, opening up and eventually breaking down. We reject, disrespect and diminish our emotions just as our father did. These suppressed emotions pile up and the desire to be loved and heard becomes a deep craving and a desire that seems impossible to achieve. Many of us are deeply sensitive individuals, deeply empathetic and emotional, which was not only turned against us, but continues to be a struggle if we keep rejecting that part of us, which many of us do until we start healing. Through completely invalidating the child, a narcissistic father creates an ideal plot for developing depression, which is directly connected to an overbearing sense of unworthiness, lack of self-love and lack of love received. This is a sad but natural response to continually not being seen and heard and living under constant pressure to be better in order to earn love. Depression arises as a result of narcissistic parenting as a whole. Since a child's feelings and needs were unacknowledged by primary caretakers and providers, and they weren't given the tools to recognize their own needs, as adults these children can feel emotionally fatigued, numb and dissociated from one's own emotions until the issue is addressed. They may find themselves unmotivated, drained, unable to cope with the world around them and in need of isolation.

Many children also suffer from anxiety as early as in kindergarten, which continues to follow them through the teenage years and later in adulthood. They were raised to be confused, repressed and were controlled from an early age which creates an inner conflict in a child as it is unable to express itself without inhibition and live in alignment with its true self because they are judged at home for it. When we are not cherished for who we are, we feel abandoned and unworthy, like somehow we don't matter, which is exactly how a narcissistic father makes their child feel.

Children of narcissistic fathers, regardless of sex, may develop sadistic or masochistic behavioral patterns, unconsciously seek pain and involve themselves in situations that don't benefit them, which further, in their mind proves their unworthiness. They may struggle with substance abuse and eating disorders and others may develop antisocial behaviors. There are cases, especially with the scenarios of golden children, where a child may become a narcissist themselves or exhibit some narcissistic traits. Being constantly put on a pedestal and given special treatment makes them believe that they are truly special and so they may seek the same validation they had from their father upon reaching adulthood. They may adopt narcissistic traits of their father and find themselves scapegoats, recreating scenarios from their childhood.

Self-doubt

Do you second-guess yourself?

Do you dwell on the past and judge yourself harshly for not doing better?

Do you constantly feel stuck in life, finding it hard to make a decision?

Constant gaslighting leaves marks and living in a constant state of numbness, being unable to go with the flow of life, second-guessing one's intuition and perception are just some of these marks. People who were raised by a narcissist commonly struggle with self-doubt, which reflects not only in their relationship with the father and family members, but transpires in other areas of life as well. The inability to trust oneself and one's own judgment makes it difficult for those people to make even the simplest decisions. Big life decisions such as choosing a college major, moving places or getting married are areas where one feels unsafe, simply because there is a lack of self-assurance and a fear of making the wrong decision. The narcissistic father usually was the one trying to impose his will onto the child and in adulthood, this creates a blockage to perceiving what feels right, what is good or bad for one's well-being. Even when a decision is made, there is a tendency to dwell on it and second-guess the choice made, especially if prior to choosing a certain direction one pops into an obstacle or a temporary setback. These setbacks are human, but someone who was raised by a narcissistic father may see them as fatal and an ultimate proof that the decision they have made is wrong.

There is a constant inner battle that takes away a lot of mental and emotional energy. You may feel constantly stuck, not knowing which way to go and not trusting yourself enough to make the decisions for yourself. There was always someone who knew better for you, so it is hard to believe that you are perfectly capable of making choices for yourself. If your father is a narcissist you may find yourself constantly swinging back and forth between decisions, not knowing what you truly want. As bizarre it may sound to others who came from healthier family environments, for someone like you and me, knowing exactly what we want can be immensely difficult. Children of narcissistic fathers frequently feel stuck between a rock and a hard place, while not knowing exactly what the rock and the hard place are. There is an extreme amount of mental pressure to make the right choice and so we may be trapped in paralysis for a very long time. The "I wish I had done that or didn't do this" thought creates a vicious circle of regret and feeds the self-doubt, expanding it even more.

The inability to love oneself

Do you think you are complicated or hard to love?

Do you expect perfection from yourself?

Have you ever thought something is wrong with you?

While self-love comes naturally to those who grew up in healthy families, when a family has a narcissist and he happens to take the main role as the head of the household, a child feels from a very young age that they are somehow strange and different from other kids, especially when they have a role of the scapegoat. Since the love they received was always conditional, they don't understand how self-love feels, believing it must be earned by accomplishing one's goals and dreams, just like the love they receive from other people is. The image of themselves their father has created lives in their subconscious, and so children of narcissists fail to see, recognize and love their talents and their own worth. I have encountered so many of them who are beyond successful and have a life many would envy them for, and yet they don't love themselves, they don't love their lives and don't celebrate their success. This is because they don't know how to. They believe that to be truly happy means to be perfect - to believe one is worthy, one needs to achieve incredible success and prove themselves to be extraordinary. Being human is not enough. Ironically enough, this *never good enough complex* creates blockages for pursuing goals that one truly cares about, while they may find themselves making other achievements relatively easy. This goes back to their father's conditioning, where one side of a child's personality was praised and the other dismissed. As a result, the dismissed part of the self can't be fully expressed and not only that - it is followed by a disbelief in one's abilities to achieve what makes their heart sing. Some are so sadly scared of failing and disappointing themselves and their family that they don't even try to pursue certain goals, which keeps them stuck for a long time.

Lack of self-love creates another loop of negative patterns, which is the loop of self-sabotage and self-blame in adulthood. I have been told countless times by my closest friends that they wish they could make me see myself the way they see me. Children of narcissistic fathers don't believe they are anyone special, and may even think everyone else is way better than them, someone who is even doing much less than they are, simply because they weren't recognized in their family as such when they were children. They not only find it hard to trust in their abilities and talents, but they find it hard to believe their own judgment. Learning how to follow the inner guide we all have is difficult, but it is even more difficult if you were raised by a narcissistic parent. Narcissistic fathers are harshly and unjustly critical and need to be in control of their children's lives. This leaves very little space for freedom of expression and thought and a lot of space for self-doubt and even self-hate. If you always see yourself in a negative light, feeling stuck in life while unable to move, this is because your parents failed to give you a valid prize and acknowledge your achievements. Many of us who had toxic upbringing fail to battle the nagging feeling of unworthiness, but that does not prove that we are actually, truly unworthy.

Unclear identity

Do you find it hard to identify and understand yourself and your needs?

Does your life feel directionless?

Do you find it hard to define who you are?

Do you feel like your identity is constantly in a crisis?

Do you feel like you don't fit in or belong anywhere?

Unclear identity is notable both in social interactions and set of personal beliefs. What comes naturally to other children may be postponed for those who were raised by a narcissistic father. You may feel as if you are endlessly floating in life. The real you was suppressed so it is natural that it is difficult to fit in and find out who you are. Your goals may frequently change. If you had goals, you may find that they don't satisfy you, which leaves a sense of emptiness. A lack of meaning and direction in life is frequent for those who were raised by narcissistic fathers, as their identity and the inner child never got a chance to be accepted and nourished. Things you did for a long period of time may not be as fulfilling and you may feel clueless as to who you are and what you want. While others stroll through life following its natural flow, children of narcissistic fathers spend a lot of mental energy trying to figure out what they want and who they are. They feel lost, struggle with a sense of belonging anywhere and may feel deeply dissatisfied about their lives, even if on the outside everything seems to be smooth sailing for them. It is not uncommon for them to feel rejected by social groups, to feel uncomfortable in their own skin and among groups. Troubles socializing, associating with others and social anxiety are some of the ways a lack of clear identity blocks one from living a fulfilling authentic life. If they were compared to other children from a young age, as adults they may continue this unhealthy habit, thinking everyone else is better than them, associating with people with troublesome backgrounds or friends who are approved by their father. Some avoid social interactions altogether due to a sense of personal imperfection and inadequacy. Others may develop social chameleon traits trying to adapt, again, due to lack of clear identity, as one does not know who they are so they may find it difficult to associate with others in an authentic manner.

You were told who you are and you were given a role, so once you are old enough to make your own choices you don't know how to free yourself from the projected ideals and given identity you took on for so long. This is a subconscious process, as we are made to believe that somehow who we truly are is something to be ashamed of and something that needs to stay in control, as no one is going to love us if we display these traits that are authentic to ourselves.

We all have the inner compass that guides us, but in this case, that compass was metaphorically taken away from us, so we could be easier to manipulate into fulfilling a destiny that is not ours to fulfill. Anger, frustration and the nagging feeling like you are running out of time are all connected to harsh conditioning and limitations you as a child received. It is very difficult for children of narcissists to understand exactly what they want, as the expectations and the pressure that was inflicted on them is in direct opposition with what the child truly desires and wants from day one. Their peers may look at them as clueless or confused, which furthermore deepens the wound their father created. Scapegoats are not the only ones who struggle with an identity crisis. Golden children too have an unclear self-image, wondering why people are not always recognizing their talents, as they were raised to believe they are special. These individuals are finding it immensely hard to be in sync with their true identities as they weren't given a chance to separate themselves from the parenting they received. What they do may seem like success and the life they live may seem fulfilling, but because they unconsciously embrace the role they were given as children, many end up feeling lost and depressed because of this inner conflict that perpetually pulls them in two different directions.

Negative self-talk

Do you feel like a failure?

Do you frequently give in to inner criticism?

Do you dwell on past mistakes and failures, while failing to give yourself credit for the success you achieved?

Do you feel like whatever you do is never good enough?

I know how it feels, I have been there. Being constantly blamed for everything that happens in your family and for things that are beyond your control results in constant-self-blame in adulthood. *I can't do this. I am not talented enough. Everyone hates me. I can never find happiness. I don't have what it takes to land that job. I am not attractive enough to find love. I am too sensitive. It is my fault that didn't work out. If I only tried harder.* You name it. Children are selfless and they are like sponges, whatever they are surrounded by they absorb. When that something is negative and blocks their growth, it soon becomes the unconscious pattern of negative self-talk we are frequently unaware of. What we are told is wrong with us becomes what we personally think needs to be fixed. We believe we are not good enough the way we are and that somehow we don't deserve all the good things in life. We believe that people who are happy must be special or somehow better than us because our parents, the father and his flying monkeys failed to be our guide and help us navigate our personal development in a healthy manner. Constantly suppressed feeling of unworthiness creates a loop of negative thoughts, as one believes they are not good enough, successful or attractive enough, seeing themselves in a negative light even when that is far from truth.

Developing a negative self-talk is a very natural response to paternal narcissism. Every conviction we had about ourselves as children internalizes and finds ways to sabotage our happiness in the future. Our father speaks through us even once we break ties with him. These false beliefs we have about who we are, how good and lovable we are, are deep-rooted and we may or may not be aware of them. Because we believed as children that we are somehow not enough the way we are, we tend to develop harsh inner critics and perfectionism, which together threaten to do even more damage to our mental health. We strive to be perfect and achieve grandiose goals, we overwork and take a lot of burdens to carry along the way while not giving ourselves credit for all the hard work we have done and even criticizing ourselves for not doing better. Negative-self talk is based on false beliefs and we are usually not aware of why we feel the way we do. And that is ok.

Social withdrawal and feelings of inadequacy

Do you feel alone in this world?

Are you deeply afraid of rejection and take criticism to heart?

Do you feel like you are not good enough to be accepted by others?

Do you feel frequent need to isolate yourself from others?

Feeling inadequate is common for us who were ignored and mistreated as children. The treatment we received from our father and our family in general leaves us feeling like outcasts. Being rejected, dismissed and discarded by those who were supposed to love us selflessly creates a belief system that is hard to shake in teenage years and in adulthood. What was once criticism and a blame game at home becomes a fear of being abandoned, rejected and judged by others when we are older. The trick to this pattern of thoughts is that we truly believe we are less than good and that something is inherently wrong with us. We try to be perfect and do our best, and so we become highly sensitive to criticism and take rejection far harder than other people do. Being rejected your whole life is something not many understand as there is a premise that family, just because you have one, is a safe and a healthy place where you can feel the most like yourself. People forget that sometimes it is our fathers who teach us to be submissive and obedient instead of building our self-confidence. If they fail to secure the base for our emotional and mental growth, later in life we may frequently experience feelings of embarrassment, shame, rejection or humiliation. The world can feel just as harsh and unloving as our father was, may leave us just as confused as he did, simply because we were manipulated and controlled from a very young age.

Many who struggled with narcissistic mistreatment in childhood frequently have a desire to hide away from the world and withdraw into a shell where no one can hurt or betray us. This shell is a protective mechanism we subconsciously created for self-preservation when we were children, and in adulthood, even when we still don't need it, we are scared to leave it behind. It is our safe zone, and because we believed that no one cares for us, we felt unlovable, invisible, inadequate or rejected by our own father we think, in the back of our mind, that the other world is as harsh and critical as he or our family was. Feeling like you don't belong anywhere and a fear that people will reject us is fairly common and a normal response to the parenting style you have received. This happens because of the merged identities and projections narcissistic fathers placed upon us, which cause difficulty in being truly open, sociable and authentic with people around us. Even when we are with people we feel isolated, distant and frequently anxious, which can lead to loneliness, feeling misunderstood and feeling rejected by peers, which is just another way in which our father's narcissism affects us without their direct involvement. Our fathers taught us that being ourselves and expressing our true thoughts, needs and desires is somehow bad or wrong and needs to be under control, and so as we grow up that gets transformed into a fear of rejection and a false belief that we can't be loved and accepted as we truly are. As a result, we struggle with anxiety and without knowing it keep on doing what our father did - we keep his tradition by unconsciously rejecting ourselves. Even those who are surrounded by a lot of people and have many friends and acquaintances, feelings of inner loneliness are still there. We either take on certain identities we believe are acceptable and try to mold ourselves to be someone we feel is acceptable and adequate, or we decide to retreat from the world, feeling deeply rejected. In both cases, we are not being authentic, and as long that feeling stays with us, the fear of abandonment, judgment, and rejection will stay as well.

Rejection and being judged by others is taken as another proof of self-unworthiness, and it is hard to cope with, as all living beings need love and nurturing to blossom. When you are stripped of that early on and it happens to continue later, you feel like moving forward in life is a very hard task. Being isolated and relating to more toxic individuals, as mentioned above, can make the healing process even more difficult, as those who have a very little support system, find it hard to extract all their strength to move forward. Although highly unpleasant and painful, it might comfort you to know that you are not alone in your loneliness because that's how we all have felt at some point or even throughout our whole lives. Again, it is yet another part of your conditioning and not a picture of who you are.

Remember that all our relationships with other individuals or groups are just a reflection of our relationships with our fathers and not a reflection of our worth and true selves. We are all likable and we all belong somewhere, it's just that finding a sense of belonging first to oneself through embracing our authenticity, and then embracing people can require detours from our original path and belief system.

Helplessness

Do you feel like you have very little control over your life?

Do you feel tired of trying to be strong and make things better?

Does life feel like a constant battle?

Do you feel like life is against you?

When your father is a narcissist, you are constantly pulled in two directions - one that is natural, true and authentic to you, and a second one which is influenced by his toxic parenting. Because he is the person you are supposed to lean on and rely on for help, just as any child, you may find that you believe his word. As you get older, develop opinions, attitudes and gain more and more independence, you feel more and more pressure without knowing why. The pressure to do something with your life. Pressure to succeed. Pressure to move, make changes and choices for yourself. And yet you feel stuck. You have a life before you and you are immobile and paralyzed. Children of narcissistic fathers often tend to feel as if they are somehow restricted to live their life to the fullest as whatever they do will never bring them favorable results. This is because of the restriction imposed on them and this helplessness is a learned helplessness, which means that it is not the reality, but a sort of mental imprisonment a child has learned to live with. Because the narcissistic father needs validation and a narcissistic supply from the child, they will restrict the child from expressing themselves and sabotage all attempts the child makes to change how they are treated. In a narcissist's eyes, a child's free will is a threat and them changing to accommodate their own child means that they no longer have the control, but it's given to the child and that is something they can't allow.

If they give in to a child's displays of affection for too long, they believe they are somehow giving their authority away. If they punish the child for too long, they are afraid to lose the narcissistic supply, so they may do something to hoover the child back. No matter if the child tries to be more considerate, patient, kind, less fussy with their father or not, the result will always be the same - the narcissistic father will always discard them. They discard because that is how they operate and there is no amount of love that can change that. Unfortunately, when we are young we don't know how narcissists operate. All we know is that whatever we do never seems to bring us the desired result or love we crave and so this discard gets internalized and becomes the feeling of helplessness and hyper-awareness of one's behavior to the point it creates deep anxiety.

We get tired of fighting for approval, better life or love and we get drained. Ultimately, when all this is combined with the fact that whatever the child does seems to never be good enough for their father, it creates a lot of angst and confusion for the child, even causing depression. As a result, they become the adult who feels broken, stuck and unable to make a change in their life. If this seems familiar to you, know that you are not alone in your feeling that whatever they do, no matter how hard you work at something, it is never going to change where you are. Matter of fact, it is a very common theme for us, children of narcissistic fathers. Because we have been controlled and hushed our entire lives, feeling like we have no control over our destiny becomes natural. You may even feel like life happens to you, not for you, and that is completely normal considering the impact your narcissist had in your life. It is and it will always be a narcissist's intention to keep you boxed in so you can obey their wishes and fulfill their ideals. You need to understand, even though you may read otherwise, that feeling of helplessness wasn't a choice you could make. It isn't a choice even now at this moment you are reading this. It is simply a pattern, that, just like other patterns, with patience, time and kindness to yourself can be broken and turned into something beautiful.

Being gaslighted, diminished, humiliated, abused or abandoned creates scars that burn even after we have done some healing. We do not choose our parents and how we are raised, so being critical of yourself for not taking charge of your own life is only going to do more damage. We have been our worst enemies and unconscious flying monkeys of our own father, contributing to our own misfortune. That is something no one deserves, and it is something that is not your fault. The next two chapters are meant to help you break free from your narcissistic father's conditioning, break free from their influence and show you the path to healing you will take at your own pace because you are beyond loveable.

Chapter 11

Breaking free from a narcissistic father

The first sign of healing from childhood wounds created by your father is acceptance. Accepting that you cannot change your childhood or your father, that what you have experienced was never your fault and it isn't something that defines you, but most importantly, accepting that your father is a narcissist.

For a very long time I felt immensely guilty for even thinking my father was wrong. I internalized every interaction we had and took on all the blame for our relationship going downhill. I remember thinking I am really selfish and overdramatic for even thinking something is his fault and, maybe if I was a better daughter and could be more flexible, he'd appreciate me more and we'd have less clashes. But here is the thing, that is exactly the pattern we talked about previously. Shifting the blame, where you are the one taking all the guilt and all the responsibility for a relationship gone bad. Then I started gaining more clarity by studying psychology and then educating myself more about narcissism, reading tons of books just like you are reading this one. From that point onwards, things started shifting for me. I find it very interesting that many of us who have dealt with some form of abuse or neglect, particularly if we were raised by narcissists, are interested in psychology. I believe we all have that inner compass that wants to find out the truth because something just feels off and we want to understand why. Self-education is the first step to breaking free from the mental prison your father has put you in. The process may not be easy, but as time goes on you go through all five stages of grief, which are denial, anger, bargaining, depression and finally complete acceptance which brings peace and relief.

Even though we may recognize we were raised by an individual who didn't have our best interest at heart, embracing the truth can be difficult, especially when we are young and still glorifying the father we thought we had, and so denial is a natural response to suspicions that your father is toxic and may not be able to give you the love and support you needed. When people grow up and realize they were raised by a narcissist, once they get into what narcissism is at its core, the first reaction is shock and the *this can't be the truth* mentality. In the beginning we make excuses and reminisce on good memories that still prove we are wrong and that what we have discovered is false. As we engage with our father, if we have the opportunity and start seeing patterns that match with our newfound knowledge, that denial shifts into aggression. We get mad at our narcissistic fathers, mad at our family members for allowing them to manipulate and gaslight us, mad at ourselves for allowing it to continue and mad at the universe for not giving us the loving family to grow up in. I remember I felt a sense of huge injustice being done to me. I was angry that unlike my peers who grew up in healthy families, I had to struggle with issues that very few of them relate to. I was angry about being in a position where I needed to heal, instead of enjoying life and being carefree. Nowadays I am glad for the lessons I have learned and I am proud of myself for getting where I am today and being proud of myself was rare when I was younger. You may shift from denial to anger, back and forth and this is called bargaining. Trying to find excuses because what you have discovered is a shock and a huge plot twist on your whole life. Once these inner battles are over, you may feel depressed and hopeless, so everything you were angry about turns into deep prolonged sadness. We have all been there and you are not alone. However long it takes, give yourself the time to grieve your childhood, and feel as angry, depressed or confused as you need to.

When the whirlpool of emotions goes away, everything falls into place. You realize you are not crazy. You haven't imagined things. There is an explanation to what you have been experiencing your whole life. Something that didn't feel right, but was hard to explain and rationalize now has a name - narcissistic personality disorder. Suddenly, you stop feeling as guilty for being an ungrateful child as you used to. It doesn't happen overnight, but the heavy weight of guilt slowly fades away as you gain more clarity. It is called acceptance.

One of the first signs that you are breaking free from your father and his impact on you is that you start not only understanding narcissism but recognizing it in people. This may bring you a sense of unsafety and even paranoia, as you may think the whole world is full of narcissists who are out to get you. This is also the first step to breaking free from long-term effects your father had on your behavior and relationship patterns, as you start eliminating toxic people from your life solely for recognizing the signs of narcissism. You clear the air and start saying no to people, but most importantly, you start understanding the role you have been playing all along, the role you had in your family that colored in all other relationships you had. Your narcissistic father may have sabotaged you in many areas, but his narcissistic ways have made you ten times more resilient and aware of your surroundings than people who did not have the chance to be raised by a dysfunctional parent. Whether you like it or not, you will be much more aware of how the human mind works, much more alert to sociopathic, psychopathic and other abnormal human behaviors and patterns that go with that. This also means that you will be much less prone to relationships with such individuals, which is a real blessing in disguise, as it will lead you to much healthier, more positive and nourishing relationships than you had in the past. This way, learning about your father's patterns and narcissism, in general, will set you free from his influence in future relationships.

The newfound clarity is the stepping stone for breaking free from your father's control and from the conditioning you unconsciously embraced. Knowing that you were raised by a mentally unhealthy individual is a hard pill to swallow, but it will help you limit or completely cut the contact with him. The best way to deal with all narcissists is to detach yourself, emotionally, mentally and physically, as much as you can. Cutting contact or keeping it to a minimum is the ideal scenario. However, in cases when you still live with your parents or you don't have the option to retreat from an unhealthy environment, the very clarity and knowing of who you are dealing with will help you see the relationship dynamically differently. You will notice that you are not as worried as you used to be about whether or not you will hurt their feelings and you will start to feel less guilty for doing things that are good or right for you. Knowledge and self-education will help you see your father from a new, more detached angle which will in turn give you more space to breathe. Now you know they want to control you and you are prepared for manipulation, accusations and gaslighting. Staying in touch with your father and your family requires a lot of self-awareness, and so if you are in contact, never forget who you are dealing with.

Narcissistic fathers will try to influence your life no matter how old you are and they will try to hoover you, blame you or dismiss you just as they did in the past. However, the difference between your childhood and adulthood will be that now you know how to successfully recognize his narcissistic patterns of behavior and therefore you will be able to observe it rather than react to it. If you are in contact, keep your privacy to yourself. Unfortunately, narcissistic parents use the trust their child has in them to manipulate and control the outcomes of their child's behavior. Staying private about your life will give them less material to use against you and less space to interfere with your life and decisions. Being distant and knowing you have to keep your greatest joys secret from your family may be sad, but it is unfortunately crucial to keeping your sanity most of the time.

You will notice that how you perceive the world around you changes. These changes in perception will lead you to a new life, where you love yourself, trust yourself and your abilities and most importantly - feel free. Something you have struggled your whole life with will slowly start to dissolve and the next chapter will be all about that - embracing your wounds, reparenting yourself and becoming your own creator.

Chapter 12

Steps to healing and rewriting your story

Finding out your father is a narcissist is not easy, and the imprint his parenting style has created may seem hard to break free from. You may feel blocked from your own destiny, unable to live your life the way you desire. We have all been there and we all go back there unwillingly from time to time, and that is ok. Matter of fact, it is completely normal. You are not a machine and there is no magic button to turn off your subconscious mind that keeps repeating your father's words. This very moment as you are reading this, I want you to give yourself the credit for trying to learn about your father, your upbringing and why you feel so blocked or lost. It takes an immense amount of courage and desire to change your circumstances for the better and to get to the point where you can say I am a child of a narcissistic father and accept that. Complete acceptance, as mentioned earlier, is the first step and probably the hardest leap to take. Know that learning is never linear and start your healing journey gently and with patience.

Everything starts with your *enough is enough, I am not tolerating being mistreated anymore. I don't deserve this treatment I am receiving and I want to be happy for a change.* If you are looking for ways to heal, it is likely that this is exactly what you have thought. This is a great sign as it means that you are stepping into your power, even if you still feel down, stuck or ashamed. While you may feel like this internally, it can be difficult to assert these thoughts and make them a reality, but with practice, learning self-love and other techniques, it becomes easier over time. Understand that some people will not be able to understand you, so don't feel discouraged if that happens. Someone who hasn't experienced narcissistic abuse from their father may be able to relate to your experience and that is ok. What matters is that you understand and relate to your experience.

Below are some of the techniques you can use to understand yourself, eliminate negative behavioral patterns that have been reinforced by your father for a long time, and then slowly replace them. Hopefully, these will give you helpful insight, enlighten your journey and lead you towards unconditional self-love.

Developing emotional intelligence

Being raised in a healthy environment creates a predisposition for what your father or people around you may have labeled you as, oversensitive. If you can describe yourself as being too emotional, too sensitive or unstable, know that first, you are not alone in that feeling, and two, the range of emotions you feel show great capacity for empathy and emotional richness not many people possess. Matter of fact, your narcissistic father may have chosen you for the role you played precisely because of your ability to empathize and feel things on a deep level. That being said, your predispositions for developing emotional intelligence are already there, so what you need to do is just find a way to swim in those emotions in a way that is natural and healthy for you. Developing emotional intelligence is about you learning that it is ok to feel, not to reject and be embarrassed about your own emotions. We all tune in to different frequencies, but people like you and me, in particular tend to be very, even hyper-aware of things around us, which causes constant emotional alertness and intense emotional reactions. This is something to be honored. Once you honor emotions, don't think about them, but instead feel them as organically as you can. We were taught to repress or be ashamed of feelings, so the important step to healing is embracing them and for many of us, learning to recognize them for what they are. Feeling and recognizing your emotions for what they are, instead of thinking them or judging yourself for feeling a certain way, is half the job done. When you know what it is that you are feeling, you can then safely find ways to manage your own responses in a way that is not limiting to you, without self-censoring or blame. Your emotions don't define you but are only your response to the experiences you have and are all human.

Counseling with a therapist, meditating, practicing mindfulness and journaling can be ways that can help you on this journey. Remember that healing an emotional body can be one of the toughest tasks, but accepting and then slowly diminishing the effects of shame, guilt and resentment is possible and it does happen when we become friends with this very important part of our beings - our feelings.

Coming to terms with your upbringing

Healing begins once you start acknowledging that your childhood is only a part of your path and not the determining element of your future. I used to see my childhood as an unfair disadvantage that held me back in life. I used to blame my father and held a lot of resentment towards him because of the way he raised me, sabotaged my growth and happiness. To a large extent, that was true, but I allowed myself to stay in the energy of anger and resentment for too long, which adds only prolonged healing and amplified negative effects that my father's narcissism created for me. You cannot change the past and you should not put the pressure on yourself to do better in the present if you still feel resentful or held back by your family history. It seems very unfair to be stripped of the basic support system and to be discarded by your own father, and even more unfair that you have to embark on the healing journey before you start to live the life you want. But that is your journey.

Accept where you came from and understand that the trials and tribulations your father put you through had nothing to do with you, your worth or how lovable you are. You don't have to forgive your father or your family for mistreating you or neglecting you, but you absolutely need to forgive yourself and see your family life as a tough journey you will come out on the top from. It is part of you and please be proud of yourself for playing whatever role you were given for so long, because it takes a lot of resilience and inner strength, to be able to do that. Enduring the narcissistic treatment from your own father is a sign of fortitude, so don't reject it, but rather stand tall. You have been through it all and yet here you are, reading this book, facing your demons and your past, trying to find your way out and through. That is courage. You were a threat to your father's sense of power, not because you are weak, but because you are powerful, so accept where you came from and own it.

Strengthening the identity

Because you were told who you should be from day one of your life, defining who you are can be a tricky task, simply because even though you may have developed interests and beliefs, it is likely that there are some that you have unconsciously adopted. These would be choices, beliefs, ideals, and ideas that you live by and have taken on, but you find them not to be as satisfying. These beliefs are those we have about ourselves and the world around us that don't serve us. Many are created as defense mechanisms, while others are incorporated in our system without us consciously being aware of them. You may feel confused about which way to go in life and that is ok. Maybe you always wanted to become an artist, but you were made to believe that you won't be successful at it, so you may have suppressed that part of your identity and refocused your attention to something your father thought was more useful. Maybe you wanted to express yourself through dressing a certain way or living an alternative lifestyle. Whatever your story may be, to heal from narcissistic damage caused by your father you need to get in touch with who you truly are. What is it that you always wanted to do but didn't because you were afraid of failure, judgment or rejection? Your father has used these fears to guide you in the direction that suits them and enables their narcissistic supply, so you need to embrace those fears and understand who they come from. It is ok to be yourself. Let go of fear and whenever you are about to do something, start asking yourself:

Will it make me happy?

Do I feel expansive when I am doing this?

Do I want to feel this way?

What will happen if I do what I feel called to do?

Do I feel like myself when doing this?

Is this really what I think or is it my father speaking through me?

How will I feel if I accept/reject this offer? Why?

Knowing who you are means rediscovering and finding lost pieces of yourself and putting the puzzle back together. The stronger the bond you have with your authentic self, the less power your narcissistic parent will have over you. Take your time to find these answers then strengthen the bond with the person you find on the other side - yourself. Please stop judging your real self, because that is what your father did for so long.

Our experience with narcissistic fathers can be very

different, so strengthening the core of your identity may be different than mine and vice versa. This can vary from learning more about who you are to completely rediscovering yourself and finding your true self. Be patient with yourself, discover yourself bit by bit and things will slowly start falling into place.

Developing positive self-talk

Replacing the *I am worthless, I will never make it, I am unlovable with I am worthy, I will make it and I am lovable* is something that takes practice, but it is achievable. Positive self-talk is based on self-love, which develops through acts of kindness to ourselves. It is when you start to matter to yourself more than someone's opinion, judgment or criticism does. It is about accepting yourself just the way you are because you are perfectly fine that way.

Practicing positive self-talk is also based on turning negative experiences into positive lessons by reversing your perception. This is possible particularly for us who were raised by narcissistic fathers, as their narcissism, whether we know it consciously or not, has helped us develop certain traits that are actually great virtues and strengths. If your father is a narcissist, you are likely very observant, curious, empathetic, hard-working and resilient. This alone makes you very capable, which is likely now how you'd describe yourself. This is because you were programmed to think your virtues are your flaws, because these virtues were twisted as they were too overbearing for your narcissistic father to deal with. Instead of praising your hard work and dedication, you were made to believe that what you are doing is average, or they may have even called you lazy. If you are observant or curious, they would say you are wasting time, call you suspicious or nosy. These are just some examples meant to show you how the way our father talked to us finds its way into adulthood and creates a loop of negative self-talk. Instead of your father calling you lazy, now you call yourself that, even when you are just taking a well-deserved break. The path to healing is understanding this, taking a moment to listen to your inner talk and then learning to stop yourself in repeating what your father has made you believe about yourself. What you need to understand, which is not easy for us kids of narcissistic fathers is that failures and mistakes don't define us. More so, they are not a validation that we aren't good enough.

Would you like someone to call you stupid, lazy, incompetent or unattractive? You absolutely would not. Even if someone calls you these names, why would you do that to yourself? You cannot control your father or anyone else, and therefore they don't have the power to tell you who you are and how good you are. They are not you, they are not in your body and they will never be. You have you. So be gentle to that person you see in the mirror, they have been through a lot and they don't need yet another negative comment from the person looking back from the other side of the glass.

If you were raised in a negative environment, building a negative image of yourself is natural. Narcissistic fathers focus on flaws and fail to give praise, so that is what we embrace ourselves. When we grow up we see only the failures, the mistakes, the bad choices and how we can never measure up to the ideals we expect from ourselves. We are so used to the negativity that we forget to see the little good things. We brush off compliments. Developing positive self-talk means reversing whatever is it that your father made you believe. Accepting and enjoying compliments and your own accomplishments. Giving yourself credit for the things you did. Put the pause on perfectionism. You don't need to be perfect to be loved. You don't need to be extremely successful to be respected, heard or seen. These are all fears projected by your father and not a reality, as you are absolutely fine and lovable just the way you are. Take the time and be compassionate with yourself as you would be with someone in need.

Choosing yourself

If you were invisible to your father and your family, you may grow up being invisible to the most important person in your life - yourself. To heal we first need to deal with our inability to say no without feeling guilty. Narcissistic fathers discourage acts of self-love and self-care as they need their children to cater to their narcissistic needs. This is why to break free it is important to learn to clearly recognize our own needs and then prioritize them. You are probably very familiar with the guilt you feel for saying no to other people's demands. As a result of being raised by a narcissist and in a dysfunctional family, we learned to be providers, caretakers, nurturers and that is the role we took on for a long time, giving the energy to people who most likely didn't deserve it. The key to healing here is reversing the focus on ourselves without feeling like we have to apologize for doing something that is good for us. You choose yourself by setting boundaries and making your own codex of behavior, the things you'll tolerate and the things you won't. Healthy boundaries will additionally push away the people who are selfishly using you and taking from you without giving back, and draw in healthy people who respect those boundaries because they respect you and your energy.

Establishing boundaries and asserting them works like a muscle. The first few times you get sore, aka you feel immensely guilty for not responding to someone and catering to their needs, but the more you do it, the better you will feel. Start small and reject invitations or requests that take your energy at the given moment. The guilt you have is coming from being ashamed of having needs because that is what your father found suitable. To have a peaceful, joyous and quality life, and to genuinely give to others, you first need to care for yourself. Every time you feel guilty for not following your gut instinct and extending yourself beyond personal limits to be there for others, remember to take a step back and put yourself first - the person who is asking for your help, energy or favor, no matter who they are, is doing the same. Ask yourself, do you do favors because you genuinely care or because deep down you want to avoid unpleasant feelings of guilt and shame? Know that there is nothing shameful about caring for yourself. It is not your responsibility to make someone else happy or miserable. They are responsible for their own wellbeing, just like you are responsible for yours. Your needs are just as valid as someone else's, no matter how bad they seem to be doing. So don't forget to choose the caring person who is always there for others over anyone else - always chose you.

Re-parenting yourself

I remember I believed for a very long time that had I been given the caring, love and nurturing in my family I would be in a much better place in life. That is true to an extent, because while our upbringing does influence how we carry ourselves through life, it isn't the determining factor, even if it doesn't seem like it at all at this very moment. Your original upbringing has caused wounding, so to heal you must re-parent yourself. Re-parenting yourself means reaching your inner child, embracing it and then teaching it love instead of fear. We are afraid we are not good enough. We are afraid we are not talented, attractive or successful enough. We are afraid we are not lovable. These fears stemmed from the treatment we received as children and the roles we took in our father's hierarchy of importance and worthiness. What can help is visualizing yourself as a child, seeing your fears, tears you have cried and how you felt. Once you can do that, the next step is treating yourself as you always wanted to be treated by your father and your family. Every time you feel anxious, sad or afraid, imagine yourself as a child. How would you comfort that child? By ignoring, judging, criticizing for screaming at it like your father did, or by making it feel safe, giving it consolation, and unconditional affection? Re-parenting yourself includes taking a step back from how you were raised, taking on and reversing the role of your dysfunctional father and giving yourself everything you needed from him, be it acceptance, love or kindness. This will include becoming visible to yourself, and treating yourself the way you wanted to be treated. This will not only make you feel safer in your own skin, but it will allow you to accept yourself the way you are, without imposing self-criticism and unrealistic expectations on yourself.

By not rejecting yourself and supporting your inner child and nurturing your vulnerabilities instead of discarding them, you are ultimately taking responsibility for yourself. You could not choose your childhood, but now you can choose yourself and you can become your own person of trust, someone you always needed and who was never there. Please remember that you already have what it takes to re-parent yourself, as otherwise you wouldn't be hoping or looking for healing and you are absolutely not alone. Re-parenting includes an immense amount of self-care and self-nurturing. It also includes getting in touch with your inner child and recognizing it's needs and understanding how it wants to express itself, which goes hand in hand with choosing yourself. Choose you, because you deserve all those beautiful things you were made to believe you are undeserving of.

If you find it difficult to cope with life's challenges and need support, I highly advise seeking the right therapy for you, talking to trusted people if you have them in your life and doing your best to take care of yourself. I want you to know that you are much more than you realize and I hope you will be able to find compassion you always needed as a child deep within yourself.

There is life after a difficult upbringing and your narcissistic father will have less impact on your life with each step you take toward healing. What awaits you on the other side is a shame-free life, a life where you understand guilt rather than internalize it and let it define you. Healing will allow you to see your father from a whole new perspective and most importantly, to see yourself in a much more realistic, positive light.

Conclusion

Paternal narcissism is an illness that impacts not on the person who has it, but more importantly and more significantly everyone else in the family, particularly children. Someone who has not experienced it as a child, will have trouble understanding it, as such fathers are masters of disguise who appear to be the best dads there are, while being immensely toxic for their children and their entire family. It is a sickness that leaves a mark on the offspring that can be hard to deal with in adulthood. The relationship a child has with a narcissistic father is based on manipulation, control, projection and blame games, so it consequently steals joy from the child's life. Narcissistic fathers sabotage freedom and take away the power from their children. Parent-child relationships with them lack in real depth a truly intimate interpersonal connection has, as a narcissist is not able to love unconditionally, but loves only with strings attached.

Narcissistic fathers are everything but protectors, although they know very well how to play that role. They, instead of supporting their child, try to diminish them, discard, ignore and abandon them when the child needs them the most. Instead of helping the child strengthen their self-confidence and personal power, narcissistic fathers prey on their child's weaknesses, as even their own children are seen as a threat to their imaginary authority and grandiosity. Children of narcissistic fathers feel used, abused, unloved and abandoned, many times without knowing why or being able to pinpoint what is it that makes them feel the way they do. This is because their fathers are gaslighting, shifting the blame and projecting, which can be very hard to spot for someone who has no knowledge and awareness of narcissistic behavior. The main damage they do lies in the misuse of their power and role of the father, which they utilize to gain narcissistic supply from their children, the family as a whole and the society.

Children who grew up with them are the ones who were not given the freedom to be children nor the freedom to be themselves. At a very young age there was a role they were demanded to play and anything that deteriorates from that role, even if it is something that makes the child happy, needed to be punished, suppressed and controlled.

The bond between the narcissistic father and their child exists, but it is unhealthy and not based on mutual respect and love, but on shame and guilt. Such a father projects his deepest fears of inadequacies, shame and rejection on their children, but they also do the same for their ambitions, unrealistic qualities, imagined authority and false sense of personal power, grandiosity and success. Based on these two they give their children the roles of the scapegoat and the golden child where the first one becomes the embodiment of the narcissistic fathers' fears and the second one becomes the embodiment of their ideals. Neither of these are based in reality and are never a reflection of a child's real potential, skill, character or talent. The scapegoated child is the one who is ultimately the greatest threat to a narcissist's false sense of self-importance, and so that child will be the one to be discarded and rejected. In homes with more children, his children may easily get abandoned for their siblings simply because they are giving the father a better narcissistic supply, are better at feeding their ego by playing out the ideals their father has, catering to him, adoring and worshiping him. In other words, equality and mutual support are not in a narcissistic father's vocabulary as he makes his children compete for his admiration, love and attention.

Narcissistic fathers poison the whole family with this competitive energy and instead of creating a safe environment for the children to grow, they turn family members against each other. The children's mother and the scapegoated child are usually the ones to blame for all the failures, mistakes and wrongdoings, particularly for those he himself has committed. His wife is described as emotionally cold, distant, unloving, unsupportive and a sabotager of his and the family happiness or she takes the role of the flying monkey, catering to his needs, adoring him and supporting his toxic parenting, many times unconsciously.

While part of good parenting includes being able to prevent deviant behaviors in children and raise happy, healthy and assertive individuals, having a father who is a narcissist means purposefully taking advantage of the fatherly role and exerting extreme authoritarianism and control over the children. They are, deep down, extremely vulnerable to rejection and criticism, are resentful and have bottled a lot of shame in a very deep corner of their subconsciousness. Such a father has no empathy, no sensitivity to their child's needs, but is observant enough to spot what these needs are and use them to gain his narcissistic supply. His children are seen as possessions that belong to him, are emotionally neglected, made to be overly codependent on him for affirmation, money or appreciation even in adulthood. Their emotional scope is very narrow and infantile, so their dealings with children are colored with aging and passive-aggressiveness, rather than maturity and openness.

Ultimately, knowing paternal narcissism opens one to perspectives many people are unaware of. While a difficult road, one can heal from the wounding caused in childhood and rise above it. In fact, that is exactly what happens in the great majority of cases for those whose father was a narcissist. It takes patience, kindness to oneself, learning about self-love, self-compassion and self-re-parenting to come out the other end, and it is not a mission impossible. Narcissistic fathers make us feel alone, isolated and rejected, so it is through healing work that we embrace who we are without continuing to do the same thing our father did - judge and criticize ourselves. It is through learning about paternal narcissism, its toxicity and the nature of interpersonal relationships that it influences that we rise above. And in the end, we truly do.

Narcissistic Mothers

The truth about the problem with being the Daughter of a Narcissistic Mother and how to fix it. A guide for healing and recovering after narcissistic abuse

Dr. Theresa J. Covert

Introduction

> **A NARCISSIST IS A CON ARTIST, THEY SELL YOU A DREAM AND DELIVER YOU A LIVING NIGHTMARE.**

Pride, arrogance, ego, and admiration; these are all feelings that are okay with some restraint. However, a narcissist is excessively proud and thinks that they are entitled to get anything that they want.

So, what is narcissism?

Narcissism has its origins in Greek mythology where there was a young man named Narcissus. He was a Greek hunter from Boeotia and the son of the river god and a nymph. He was a remarkably handsome person.

One day, Nemesis lured him to the edge of a lake where he fell in love with the water pool reflection of himself. Narcissus was so engrossed with admiring his reflection that he ended up drowning in the lake.

In this day and age, narcissism is a theory used in psychoanalysis; the psychoanalysis theory has its beginnings in the 1914 essay on narcissism by Sigmund Freud.

Also, the American Psychiatrist Association classifies narcissism as a mental disorder characterized by patterns of need for the admiration of others and a lack of empathy for others, a grandiose sense of self-importance and a sense of entitlement.

Narcissism is a personality trait disorder. Most psychologists and psychoanalysis experts agree that narcissism is a cultural and social problem that is on the increase in our world today.

However, most specialists in the field of psychology agree there is healthy narcissism; these specialists see healthy narcissism as a show of healthy self-love, and most experts also agree that the line between healthy self-love and narcissistic propensities is an extremely thin one and that healthy self-esteem can rapidly grow into narcissism without an individual's knowledge.

An obsession over one's physical appearance, traits, and achievements at unnatural levels can lead to a distraction from daily life and activities.

Narcissism Personality Disorder (NPD) is one of the three dark personalities together with Machiavellianism, and Psychopathy. These three dark personalities are referred to as the "dark triad." People with these three disorders exhibit malevolent qualities.

It will help at this point not confuse narcissism with egocentrism. Narcissists are all about their egos, just like the egocentrics, but there is a difference between a narcissist and an egocentric person. A narcissist only gets their fix of admiration or whatever supply it is that they need for the moment from someone else.

Dealing with narcissism is very difficult; this is because the people suffering from it do not see it as a problem. The people who suffer from narcissism believe that they are perfectly fine and healthy.

Any event or person that forces people living with Narcissistic Personality Disorder to double-check themselves will not produce change. They will still try to cover the facts about them as attacks and live on with their disorder.

Chapter 1
Narcissistic Personality Disorder

> **THE BEST TEST TO SEE IF SOMEONE IS A NARCISSIST, SAY NO TO THEM AND WATCH THEIR RESPONSE.**

Most experts in the field of psychiatry believe that Narcissistic Personality Disorder (NPD) cannot be cured. This means that people diagnosed with it will have the symptoms of the disorder all their lives and will have to continually work hard to deal with the behavioral difficulties caused by the disorder.

Although people diagnosed with NPD might experience relief of symptoms and might learn valuable coping strategies, they will still have some signs of the disorder for the rest of their lives. Also, most psychiatrists don't believe that medication works well to control any personality disorder, especially NPD.

Narcissism is a kind of belief a person has about themselves, that they are unique and more important than others around them. With this belief, they often act in particular ways and will do things to boost their image in the eyes of others.

The belief in their superiority over others is so deeply

ingrained in narcissists that they experience many difficulties when dealing with other people as they will often treat everyone else as less important.

Narcissistic Personality Disorder (NPD), therefore, is the term that connotes a type of mental disorder wherein the individual affected has an exaggerated sense of self-importance.

Individuals affected with NPD have a deep need for reverence from others, though they lack empathy for others. Individuals affected with NPD do not present themselves for psychological treatment because they do not see that there is an issue with their conduct, even though they are aware that people around them constantly find them very difficult to deal with.

The criteria officially used for diagnosing Narcissistic Personality Disorder are described in the Diagnostic and Statistical Manual, Version Five (DSM-V). The DSM-V is the book mental health experts use to diagnose mental illnesses.

It is pertinent to note that some people might display signs of narcissistic tendencies but do not have full-blown NPD.

A few criteria for diagnosing NPD as described in the DSM-V are:

A. Antagonism, characterized by Grandiosity, and

B. Attention seeking.

The criteria described in the DSM-V can be explained through the actions of the particular individual suffering from NPD. An individual who is affected by

NPD will only think of themselves. Their actions will reveal that they think only about themselves and seek to put down individuals around them.

For instance, an individual suffering from NPD may misrepresent their contribution to a work project while deprecating the commitment of a co-worker to the project. The individual might even steal the ideas of others and take credit for the ideas and actions of others. An individual suffering from NPD must be at the center of the universe at all times.

To be diagnosed with full-blown NPD means that a person must exhibit this attention-seeking behavior both over time and in many different circumstances. They must have exhibited it as a young adult, and they must have grown older without much change in their behavior. They exhibit attention-seeking with their family, at work, and in the community. This personality trait seems stable, no matter who they are with and what they are doing.

A person suffering from NPD cannot have their behaviors explained based upon how old they are. For example, many teenagers act like they are the center of the universe and may exaggerate their actions, but this can be explained as a normal stage in their psychological growth, which they will eventually outgrow. However, a person with NPD will never abandon their teenage behaviors. So for an adult, some acts are not considered normal. This is one of the reasons why personality disorders such as NPD are not diagnosed until a person is an adult.

Someone with NPD will seek attention and have a false

sense of self no matter what their state of sobriety is. For instance, a person who behaves like a narcissist while drunk, but is a loving and healthy person while sober, would not be diagnosed with NPD because their behaviors are as a result of the alcohol in their system. Someone with NPD will act like a narcissist no matter what their state is.

Taken as a whole, when someone has NPD, they believe that they are the center of the universe and everything revolves around them and as such, they bear no regard for the feelings of people around them, along with the fact that they will not be empathetic with other people.

People suffering from NPD will do whatever they can to be the center of attention and show others how significant they are to the world. They will continue to show these traits throughout their whole lives. Usually, these traits start to show in their lives during adolescence, and they will carry these traits into adulthood.

It is estimated that up to 6.2% of the general population suffer narcissistic personality disorder and that men are more than twice as likely to be diagnosed as women.

How Narcissistic Personality Disorder Develops

As with any other mental illness or personality disorder, there are different explanations for NPD. The causes of NPD could show up independently or exist along with one another in someone's life; this will then encourage the development of NPD.

The first puzzle piece in the development of NPD is genetics. If a family member had NPD, it is quite likely that children and some other relatives might also develop the disorder. This is because of psychobiology; the idea that the brain and human behaviors are connected. If the brain is genetically wired in one way because of the genes a person has inherited from parents and grandparents, then a person is likely to inherit the genes that caused for the wiring to occur in such a way to create NPD. People who have a genetic predisposition are more likely to suffer from NPD than those without it.

The other trigger for NPD is parenting issues. If a person lives with a parent or in a family situation where they are overly pampered, treated continuously as unique, or given everything they ever ask for without any idea that there are limits, they are more likely to develop NPD. Children need boundaries and discipline, and without them, they will grow up with an unrealistic view of both themselves and how the world works. They incorporate the belief that they are special and perfect into their worldview.

On the other hand, people who grew up with parents who were especially harsh and never valued anything the child did can also develop NPD. The child develops a defense mechanism to offset the negative and constant criticism that they receive. Think of it like a pendulum swinging the other way. If the parent is overly harsh to the child, the child will start to overcompensate by believing that they are entitled to everything, that they are special, and that they deserve the world, just to combat the negativity that surrounds them every single day. This is generally thought to happen because the child may be overcompensating to try to prove their worth to their parent. They want to earn the parent's love and approval.

No matter which type of parent the person with NPD had, the parental behaviors began while the child was young, generally before the age of three.

A third factor that may be relevant to the development of NPD is society's ideas of who and what is important. For example, the idea that the most powerful, rich, and successful are more important than "ordinary people" has become an ingrained belief thanks to mass media's preoccupation with these types of people. In watching reality TV, people who are self-centered, selfish, and rude to others are idealized, whereas people who are caring and compassionate are often marginalized or completely ignored. Second, people receive more approval from outside influence when they are smarter, more prosperous, or have a higher status. This could cause people to work for this higher status so they can receive the same type of recognition. Last, there is a weakening of the community in our society. Children are not often brought up to believe they are part of something bigger than themselves, which leads to kids having more difficulty identifying with others. A grandiose self-image replaces their ability to empathize.

Usually, however, there is a mixture of both genetic factors and environmental factors, both personal and societal, at work with the development of any personality disorder. If a parent or other close family member has the personality disorder, the child will likely grow up both with a genetic link to get it and in an unstable home environment where the traits are more likely to develop. Because many of the traits have been shown to exist since childhood, it is easy to see why the disorder becomes so challenging to treat.

However, that doesn't mean there are not treatments or options for a person suffering from NPD or their families. The next chapter will give some clues into the current treatments available through modern medicine and psychiatry to handle Narcissistic Personality Disorder.

You will, undoubtedly, have heard of the term 'Ego'. It is naturally assumed that everyone has one; although some people's egos are much larger than others. Ego is an idea of your self-worth; in many people, this is a fragile item; easily affected by others and their opinions and views.

Your ego will be built upon your own beliefs and experiences throughout life; if you have always met with success, you are likely to have a bigger ego and be more confident. Likewise, those who often meet with failure will tend to have a diminished ego and be less confident in their abilities. Everything you undertake in life will help to build or diminish this ego; it is a moving, almost living thing, and this is an essential, healthy part of life.

Egoism is an extension of this principle; it believes that all actions and goals should relate to yourself; everything that you do should benefit you and help you to reach your own goals. Moving a stage past this and you become someone with NPD; when the achievement of your goals and the benefit of your actions focuses entirely on you. This should be regardless of the effect on those around you. Egoism is often disguised as kindness and generosity; giving someone else a gift without a reward can seem selfless; in fact, it is often a tool used by someone with NPD to manipulate and gain the support of others; the gift can later be mentioned to ensure a favor is provided when needed. A true egotist will not consider the thoughts of others; their interests lie only in what is good for them.

An ego which centers on your own needs above all others is essential for the creation of NPD. What is perhaps the most interesting thing about this is that it is agreed that someone is born without any ego. At the moment you are born, you do not have any preconceived ideas about the world, yourself, or even any knowledge. All these things are built upon from the moment you are born. Your first instincts will be to reach out and explore the world around you; in a baby, this is done through the senses; sight, touch, smell; hearing, and taste. At this point your ego is simply a reflection of what others think and do; if they praise you and smile at you then you will feel good about yourself, if they do not, you will feel bad about yourself. From this simple beginning, your ego will grow and will be fed by the images and experiences around you. From this standpoint, an egotist or someone likely to have a narcissistic personality is a product of society. Of course, this is a very simplistic approach as there are many other factors which will influence the development of NPD; the exact cause is not known but could be linked to your genes.

The definition of egoism is that the self-belief created by your ego is essential to ensuring you make the correct moral decisions and, therefore, behave by accepted moral standards.

Of course, these standards also extend to assist in understanding the development of NPD; egoism accepts that anyone should put themselves first and this self-belief should motivate all conscious actions; this means that self-interest is an acceptable conclusion to any action, which is exactly what someone with NPD does!

Selfishness is also a trait of someone with NPD; their desires are placed above all others. They see themselves as more important and worthy of success than anyone else, and this becomes a justification for being selfish. Almost everyone has been selfish at some point or the other in their life; it could be hanging onto a vital person because they need them rather than it being the best thing for the person or the relationship. Alternatively, it could be something more straightforward, like taking the last chocolate!

However, the traits of selfishness are sometimes essential in parts of life. Business leaders, in particular, need to put the interests of their company first to succeed. This can even be seen to be essential for preserving the jobs and welfare of their employees. However, putting the company's needs first will also ensure that their own needs are being given priority. The very traits which are essential for business success can start someone on the course to a narcissistic personality even if they do not develop NPD.

The economic acceptance of selfishness as an essential

trait if the business shows the complications which arise when trying to establish the parameters and definition of someone suffering from NPD; in many walks of life their behavior will be akin with an extremely successful person. By this logic, selfishness is a desirable and even essential trait for those who wish to succeed.

To be genuinely selfish you need to be devoid of empathy or consideration for other people's feelings; this is, perhaps, the critical point at which someone will change from being considered socially 'normal' and having a personality disorder. Anyone who has NPD will be unable to establish empathy with those around them; this inevitably leads to the ability and desire to manipulate those around you as you lose the ability to respect their feelings or needs. This type of behavior is associated with those suffering from NPD as well as psychopaths.

It must be understood that, as with all personality traits, it is essential to have an awareness of self and to look out for your interests. Being selfish is necessary at times to ensure you stick to your principles, values, or simply to complete a job close to your heart. The crucial difference is understanding the effect this may have on others and choosing to do it anyway, despite the emotional and physical consequences. If you are never selfish, you will never stand up for anything you believe in and will be likely to spend your life following the herd, possibly never achieving your full potential.

It has been suggested that selfishness in adults can be created through a difficult childhood. Any child who has little or no praise or even acknowledgment of their existence is likely to retreat into their world. Some of these children will become recluses and socially inept for life; others will build their fantasy worlds to retreat into and escape the harshness of their life. These fantasy worlds will often revolve around having the control, power, and admiration that they are not receiving as a child. These worlds can be carried into adulthood, and a narcissistic personality will develop as the desire to be appreciated will eclipse all other feelings. Again, this development will be in conjunction with other influences and your genes.

Selfishness is a trait of someone with NPD; however, you can be selfish without having NPD. Aside from the healthy form of selfishness which has already been discussed; most people find themselves being selfish because of the demands and stresses of their own lives; it is not a fundamental desire to hurt others but rather a reaction to your environment. Selfish people tend to come across as selfish, while people with NPD are charming and will appear to fit in well, while being very accommodating. This is because they are manipulating and controlling people around them to obtain their own selfish needs. The difference in personality is both easy to spot and an essential part of the difference between someone who has NPD and someone who does not. After all, someone who truly has NPD will be very concerned with looking good to others; this will ensure they get the help they need to achieve their goals. They will appear trustworthy and unselfish when, in fact, they are the exact opposite; the problem is their charm and charisma will hide their true personality and motivation from you.

Chapter 2
Types of Narcissism

While we talk about narcissism in general terms, there is more than one type. In the real world, when you meet a narcissist face to face, there may be signs that match the way a narcissist behaves because most of the time, they are a mix of the various types. As with typical combinations, there is always the dominant type mixed with another.

To help you to determine which one is what, here's a brief rundown of each different type and their specific characteristics or personality traits:

Cerebral

A cerebral narcissist believes that they are better than anyone and that their intelligence far exceeds that of anyone else. They flaunt their intelligence and self-assumed superiority to be admired and envied by the rest. They know everything about, well, everything. They make it a point to have an opinion or suggestion for everything that you might throw at them. They will be happy to tell you stories that show off their sheer brilliance, whether the stories are real or just made up. They are pleased to point out everyone else's failings and will look down on and sneer at anyone who is of lower intelligence. Such people are so obsessed with their grey matter that they will go out of their way to take alarmingly good care of it, sometimes to the extent that it reflects badly on their health and physical prowess. Narcissism is very often associated with sexual stimulation. Cerebral narcissists rarely engage in sexual stimulation with others, as they prefer personal stimulation over the real deal. Therefore, it would not come as much of a surprise when I say that they prefer the anonymity and lack of intimacy that comes with pornography.

For this reason, they may choose porn over real close relationships. Besides maintaining a relationship with such people is a Herculean task in itself as they will always insist on being the intellectually superior one in the relationship and assume the right to control the other person's thoughts, emotions, and actions. Even then, these relationships will be extremely short-lived as they are continually looking for more superior people to associate with. Cerebral narcissists should not be confused with somatic narcissists.

Somatic

Somatic narcissists are more closely in touch with the Greek legend of Narcissus. They are all consumed by how beautiful they believe they are. You will often find somatic narcissists at a gym or somewhere else where they are working on their appearance. For them, it is all about their body and physique. They can be seen continuously flexing their muscles and bragging about their success in sporting events. They expect their body to be the source of their narcissistic supply and so they dress up immaculately and keep themselves well-groomed. Their narcissistic supply comes from how others react to how they look or from their sexual conquests – indeed, most somatic narcissists will have a long list of partners. They never cease to boast about their conquests in bed. Even though they may have bedded many partners, most of the sex is bound to be cold and emotionless. Eventually, the word partner begins to lose meaning, and they may be more aptly described as the victim. Cheating in marital life is something that you shouldn't put past a somatic narcissist. He is happiest when his narcissistic supply comes from multiple sources. They are quite dangerous as they know how to manipulate people both emotionally and through sexual intercourse. This tends to scar their spouse for life if they decide to be in a long-term relationship with them.

Overt

This form of narcissism manifests in grandiosity. They are preoccupied about having outstanding success in many areas, like brilliance, attractiveness, sense of power, ideal love, etc. Since they have an immense sense of grandiosity, they believe that they can only be fully appreciated by other people on their level of grandiosity. The overt narcissist always has to be in control of any situation. They are never wrong, and they will never be shy about making it clear that everything is about them and that everything has to be done the way they want it done. Their egos are super-sized, and they are not backward in showing it to you either. The overt narcissist can cut you up, physically or verbally and will not show a single second of remorse or guilt. Such people are interpersonally very exploitative and will not think twice before using someone to achieve their own needs. Although very arrogant on the inside, they are experts at masking their egotism within a false humility. They envy other people to a great extent and get jealous of their achievements, possessions, and relationships. They seriously lack empathy, and this makes them unfit to work in a group. They are usually loners.

They may be seen as being overconfident, and they are extrovert in their behavior – in fact, it would be easier to describe their personality as loud, noticeable, larger than life, and somewhat oppressive.

Covert

The covert narcissist exhibits all the normal traits you would expect to find in a narcissist but with one difference: they want someone to take care of them. They are best described as the shy form of narcissism. He has grand fantasies similar to other types of narcissists, but he lacks the drive to pull it off successfully. He is too timid to get what he wants and lacks self-confidence. He usually feels worthless at not being able to pull off exactly what he wanted. He faces large feelings of shame about the same thing. He rarely takes credit for his achievements. He openly admires successful people and secretly envies them. He is unlikely to accumulate appropriate friends and prefers to surround himself with inferior persons. Such people are hyper-vigilant to rejection and humiliation. They could be described as parasites, living off other people. They will typically exhibit some signs of an illness that needs taking care of, and that is why they can never be what you want. They don't want to take responsibility for anything and will look for a partner who is strong, successful, and intelligent, one that can run their lives while they don't need to contribute anything. Covert narcissists will sometimes pair up with the overt narcissist.

Unprincipled

The unprincipled narcissist does not have a conscience and cannot seem to tell the difference between what's right and what's wrong. They care very little about laws, values, and conventions and stay just within the boundaries of the law. They exploit others without the slightest bit of remorse because they consider other people as inferior to them anyway. This unprincipled lifestyle makes them more than willing to risk harm, and they are remarkably fearless in the face of danger. Their malicious and diabolic tendencies are easily visible, and get them into trouble with the authorities. They achieve gratification by dominating and humiliating others. These people never form an allegiance with anyone and so move from person to person with remarkable ease. They are alien to emotional attachments and do not feel the slightest remorse on ending an auspicious relationship. The people they leave crumpled in their wake are very adversely affected, as the narcissist is usually very charming. These narcissists are exceptionally dangerous because, for them, truth is only relative. They are masters of manipulation and deceit. They are very adept at scheming beneath a polite and civil veneer. Their plans are usually very cunning and worthy of admiration even though the means is hardly justified. They show no concern for other people's welfare, have no morals, scruples, and are highly deceptive when they deal with others. They will give off an air of arrogance and are driven by a need to get the better of everyone, to prove that they are smarter than everyone. This kind of narcissist may be found in prisons or drug rehabilitation centers, although there are an awful lot of unprincipled narcissists who never come up against the law. When in the vicinity of an unprincipled narcissist always be sure to keep your guard up. They smell insecurities a mile away and can easily turn you into a scapegoat for their next exploit.

Amorous

Amorous narcissists tend to be erotic or seductive in nature, and they measure their entire self-worth around their sometimes many sexual conquests. Their relationships are often pathological and, as soon as they seduce someone, they are likely to throw them to one side while they look for their next conquest. They are never looking for an emotional connection but rather seek to inflate their already bloated ego by sexually dominating other people who they consider as trophies. The victim has more or less no idea that they are being used and sometimes they sincerely fall in love with the narcissists. However, the narcissist genuinely lacks any empathy and will throw them away like paper towels. This makes them outrageous heartbreakers. Not only are they often known as heartbreakers, but they will also do some outrageous things, like pathological lying, conning their sexual partner out of money and other fraudulent acts. They use their sexual prowess to con unsuspecting people. The amorous narcissist is compensating for deep-rooted feelings of inadequacy. In most cases, they get away with it too because people hesitate to complain about them.

Compensatory

Compensatory narcissists are continually looking for a way to compensate for things that happened in the past, perhaps in their childhood, and they do this by creating an illusion that they are superior. They tend to live in a fantasy world where they play the leading role in a theater that doesn't exist rather than living a real life. They imagine achievements in a bid to enhance their self-esteem. They need an audience filled with people who will believe their deceptions, and they are extremely sensitive to how other people perceive them, looking for signs that they are being criticized. They try to compensate for everything that they feel they were deprived off. Their agenda is similar to the other narcissists except that they are more focused rather than being guilty of random acts of narcissism.

Elite

The elite narcissist is, in many ways, very similar to the

compensatory narcissist in that they are obsessed with their self-image. The sense of self they create rarely resembles the real person, but they manage to convince themselves and others that they have unique abilities and talents. They will, more often than not, turn a relationship into a contest or a competition where the only goal is to win, to prove to others that they are truly superior. This will happen with any relationship, be it family, work, or love. The elite narcissist is a social climber and will be happy to step on anyone who gets in his or her way. In a way, he is the most dangerous of all the types as he hides in plain sight so effectively that even the ones closest to him perceive him as a good and honest person. An elite narcissist is usually a highly successful businessman or businesswoman who has a very reputable profile. They consider material wealth and assets as a primary objective over real emotion. They are masters of deception and often use their talents to walk over other people. Being as cunning as they get, they usually have a legitimate and reputed business that they use as a front for all of their shady dealings. They are incredibly protective of their personal space. If they get the slightest hint that you are a threat to everything that they have built up, they will eliminate you without a second thought. They are ruthless and without remorse or empathy. They are concerned only with their well being and the achievement of their goals. They will go to any length to achieve what they want.

Below are some of the narcissistic sub-types. These sub-types can be encountered by various people daily. Some can be annoying but tolerated, while some can cause emotional harm.

Conversational

Ever recall an instance where you are talking to a certain person, ranting, or just randomly telling one of your everyday life stories to him? What's unforgettable is how the conversation always manages to end up with him as the subject and the victor? Annoying, right? Not only is it sickening to hear stories with always the same triumphant result, but it is also annoying that they always make you forget what you are about to say due to their constant interruption.

This kind of conversation can happen between normal people as well, but it is almost always the case with people suffering from narcissism. There is an even more aggressive conversational narcissist where they rudely cut you off while you were saying something, so that they can insist their own story whose lead character is always them.

If, by reading this part of the book, you are reminded of that one person who never fails to do this every time you are having a conversation, try to observe. Check out his other mannerisms, habits, or the way he behaves with other people. Chances are, you have a narcissist who is sneakily turning all his friends into his supply sources.

Group Narcissism

Whenever the topic is narcissism, we are always presented with the idea that it is all about a person who cares for nothing else but himself. This is true, but it does not necessarily rule out the possibility of narcissism that can occur in a group.

In group narcissism, the narcissist individual is always a part of the group. Usually, the group is made up of narcissist people who mirror themselves and they don't encounter any problem with having to co-exist with each other. They tend to become the narcissist supply source of each other, and you will know that it is working out as the group acts as a narcissistic entity.

You see, narcissists tend to gather or join each other in groups because it brings them comfort. This is because they are all pretty much similar, and share the same behaviors or habits. There's no questioning about why he behaves this way, and she behaves that way because they all know that they are trying to protect something deep inside them.

Now, this group becomes a protector of the hidden real selves of each member. While this looks nice and beneficial for the narcissist, this does not mean that they are already safe from the danger of self-destruction. It's always there, just below the surface.

Aggressive or Malignant Narcissism

This type of narcissism is your lesser type (like classic, cerebral, somatic, elite, and others) kicked up a notch because it becomes violent and psychopathic. Take Adolf Hitler or Ted Bundy. They can be categorized as aggressive types of narcissists.

Not all narcissists prefer to harm their supply source or victims physically. Most of the time, they just torture or abuse you mentally. However, when a narcissist becomes a bit too physical and performs the murder, the rape, or some other crimes with cold blood, that person can already be categorized as a malignant or aggressive narcissist.

Destructive Narcissism

So we have labels for, pretty much, every type of narcissist out there. Honestly, some psychiatrists do not exactly agree with these labels because identifying a narcissist is more than just knowing all the types and matching the behaviors or signs dominant to that type.

What is more, some narcissists are too clever that they can compensate for some of the behaviors to cover them up. That way, fewer tracks means less disruption to the facade that took them years and so many lies to build and complete.

Some people cannot also be classified as narcissists but they match some of a narcissist's description. Now, why am I saying all these? This is because of this type, the destructive narcissist, is one of those who do not technically fit the definition of a narcissist, but they also inflict pain on themselves and also shows general narcissist patterns.

Out of all the types, the destructive narcissist is the one that seems to be a bit irregular. They have some of the traits that can easily identify them within the various types of the narcissist, and all the while lacks some narcissistic traits that will solidify their being categorized as a narcissist.

Destructive narcissists usually have the most intense characteristics that a narcissist can have. These characteristics will ruin and destroy people around the narcissist, and because of this, you can easily associate them with a pathological narcissist. However, the mentioned characteristics are fewer.

Sexual Narcissism

While this may raise your eyebrows as we have come to know that narcissists aren't exactly crazy about having sex with someone else, let us take a quick look at who these sexual narcissists are. Sex, when blended with grandiosity, becomes sexual narcissism. A sexual narcissist boasts pleasurable sexual skills, has a sexual entitlement, and he also lacks sexual empathy.

The meaning? You get to have intercourse with a sexual narcissist, but as always, it is for his pleasure and not yours. You may feel a satisfaction, and this is no wonder because of the sexual skills of the narcissist. However, if the narcissist feels that he is already satisfied and you aren't yet, even if you are right in the middle of it and he wants to stop, he will stop.

He will only do it with you when he feels like it. So if a sexual narcissist doesn't feel like doing it, even if two weeks have passed already, you will not get any sex.

Another thing that you have to know about sexual narcissists is that they have a big tendency to be an unfaithful partner. Big surprise! Since they feel like they have all the sexual skills, they also feel that they can do it with anyone as long as they are in the mood for it.

Acquired Situational Narcissism (ASN)

This narcissism sub-type is a lot different from the rest of the types, even the main ones, as ASN is acquired later on in life as an adult. All other narcissism types are acquired in the childhood phase of a person's life.

ASN can't just happen to anyone. One needs to have the narcissistic tendency as a child for ASN to be successfully triggered. This type of narcissism is triggered when an adult with a narcissistic tendency suddenly comes across wealth, celebrity-status, or fame. Through this, the previous tendency suddenly blooms into a full-blown narcissistic personality disorder complete with signs, symptoms, behaviors, and more harmful probabilities like the usual type of narcissism. The only difference is the age when the sufferer acquired it.

What feeds their narcissistic cravings are their fans, supporters, people around them, their fake friends, assistants, social media, and the traditional type of media.

Chapter 3
How to Recognize A Narcissistic Mother

> You are not responsible for your mother's happiness (and you never were).

There is a narcissistic personality inventory (NPI) tool based on forced choice questions meant for measuring narcissism in populations of people and a diagnostic tool called the Millon Clinical Multiaxial Inventory (MCMI) used more for individual cases that can be and often are used by medical professionals to diagnose NPD (narcissist personality disorder). These tools can be helpful, but they cannot be used by themselves. They must be used in conjunction with observations of patient behavior. In order to be diagnosed and get treatment for NPD, a patient's condition should meet the criteria for a diagnosis of NPD as defined in the Diagnostic and Statistical Manual of Mental Disorders (DSM-5).

NPD Behavioral Characteristics

The manifestations of narcissist personality disorder are an extreme (some even call it erotic) self-interest that often involves an emphasis on physical appearance. If one is diagnosed with narcissistic personality disorder (NPD), it will generally result as a consequence of a psychiatrist or other qualified health professional observing the patient behaving as if he or she is without the capacity to love anyone but themselves. Most of the time, they are unable to provide their significant other, friends, and other family members with the love, friendship, and caring they all need for a healthy two-way relationship.

Also, the patient exhibits a behavior totally lacking in empathy, disregarding other people's feelings, and ignoring what others in their life care about. They have never "felt anyone else's pain" or even tried to empathize with someone going through a difficult time. In fact, there is only one perspective in the world that exists to the narcissist: their own.

With NPD the narcissist will often have an unrealistic and "out of touch with reality" overconfidence and vanity. They will view their appearance and capabilities as far better than they actually are yet they are unable to deal with even the slightest of criticism. They will hunger for and even demand praise and admiration from those in their life.

Other People Live to Meet the Needs of The Narcissist

Relating to an early paper by Martin Buber referred to earlier in this book, Buber recognized that narcissists view other people as objects to be used for achieving their ends rather than treating people as equal human beings. They will use others to achieve their own ends without the slightest thought of what it may cost the other person.

A Lack of Appropriate Boundaries

This "people are objects to be used" attitude can create a bizarre situation whereby the narcissist cannot distinguish between himself or herself and others. So the narcissist views others as an extension of themselves and think that others exist only to meet their needs. If it turns out that the other people in their life do not exist for this purpose, then the narcissist doesn't even recognize their existence.

That's right! Other people don't even exist in the mind of the narcissist if they are not living to meet every need of the narcissist. This is called the lack of the ability to recognize boundaries. In other words, other people are extensions of themselves and are expected to behave the way the narcissist expects them to and live up to every one of their expectations. There is no boundary between the narcissist and others. For those that the narcissists view as true extensions of themselves, they heap on unwarranted flattery and admiration to maintain the affirmation of their unrealistic and inflated self-worth.

Oblivious

Another behavior of the narcissist is a lack of awareness and insight. They have no idea they have a mental illness and are totally unaware of the impact their behavior has on others. This can make it very difficult to treat narcissists. This also makes it nearly impossible for them to have normal relationships with other people. All of their interaction with the other people in their lives is focused on themselves, making the continuation of any kind of favorable two-way relation that they start extremely difficult for the other person.

Lack of Appropriate Emotion

The narcissist cannot feel appropriate relational emotions because their life is not about others...it's only about them. So not only do they not have normal love emotions, but they also either repress totally or never really feel emotions like regret when they should. After hurting someone else emotionally, even committing acts of violence, when they should feel shame and remorse they do not. They live a life never apologizing, asking for forgiveness or for that matter, even feeling bad about hurting other people emotionally or physically.

Conversely, when someone does something for them that is extraordinary, and a person would normally feel the emotion of gratitude and thank them appropriately, the narcissist will not express gratitude. This is because everyone in the narcissist's life is expected to do wonderful things for the narcissist and it's not "normal" when they don't. In fact, as we will explore next, the emotion that is most likely felt when there is a lack of pandering and admiring the narcissist is injury and rage.

Observing Narcissistic Behavior

Because of the ridiculous self-image the narcissist holds so dearly they will exhibit certain characteristics inherent with the disorder. First of all, they will have a body language that can be called high and mighty, arrogant, conceited, or snooty. They will also be unbelievably overconfident, lie about things they have accomplished that they have not accomplished and pretend to be more important than they obviously are.

All of The Bragging Rights Belong to the Narcissist

They are braggarts to the extreme. Their bragging can be subtle and crafty so as not to be obvious and blatant about it, attempting to avoid getting caught in exaggerations. They can become very good at the "skill" of bragging. The bragging will be determined and unrelenting. If they do have provable achievements, they will always exaggerate the importance of the achievements they can prove. They will always act as if they are an expert at many things even if they do not know the slightest thing about the subject.

The Narcissist Is A Magical Thinker

At times the narcissist will display what you might call magical thinking about just how wonderful they are, what they know, and what they can accomplish. They even will sometimes think that just because they believe something to be correct and true that it is in reality, correct and true, even if there is strong evidence to the contrary. If it is obvious that the narcissist cannot "measure up" to someone else, they will often be envious and show disdain for and disapproval of the person to diminish them as much as possible.

The Entitled Narcissist

According to the narcissist, he or she is entitled to get everything they want and are entitled to have every event in life go their way. They are entitled to the most favorable treatment wherever they go, and everyone needs to comply with their wishes, their way of doing things and their way of thinking. They are always the special person in the relationship and not going along will classify the non-complier as a difficult or dumb and awkward person in the narcissist's special world.

The Manipulating Narcissist

Often times, other people will be forced into a subservient position by way of being an employee, spouse, or child. Alternatively, sometimes the other person will just be timid and afraid to challenge the will and authority of the narcissist. The narcissist will start each new relationship assuming the other person is in a subservient position even when they are not. This puts the narcissist in a position of easily exploiting all who are unfortunate enough to find themselves in this position.

Narcissists of Many Colors

These behaviors and attitudes are what define the mental condition of the narcissist. The condition can assume varying degrees of severity. Some narcissists have such dysfunctional family and social relationships they end up alone, broken and unable to function in society. Others can master manipulation strategies and techniques so well that they become very successful in business or end up at the top of their very demanding professions finally accumulating an "entourage" of subordinates that take care of their every need, pander to their ego, swallow their pride and usually take their very substantial paychecks to the bank. However, narcissists usually fail at one thing in life. They fail at lasting relationships where love defines behavior because they only love themselves. They have a lifelong love affair with themselves and are "forever gazing into the pool at their own reflection".

Chapter 4
Behaviors of a Narcissistic Mother

> **YES, YOU ARE LOVABLE, YOU JUST GAVE YOUR LOVE TO SOMEONE WHO DOESN'T UNDERSTAND LOVE.**

The child with Narcissistic Personality Disorder enters into adulthood with this disorder, which makes forming relationships difficult and impedes satisfaction. They are constantly subjected to internal conflict and always depend psychologically on others. The child is not an object of love that is raised consciously and selflessly; far from it. The child of the narcissistic mother is a mirror by which to gaze at and admire or deplore her.

Narcissistic mothers tend to fall into two basic classifications: smothering mothers and negligent mothers, both of which are discussed in detail below.

Smothering Mothering

The smothering mother, also known as the engulfing mother, cannot determine the boundaries between mother and daughter. The daughter is an appendage of the mother's self in her mind. What is a natural inclination from birth through the toddler stage becomes a problem later when the child is seeking autonomy. It happens surreptitiously, perhaps unconsciously on the part of both actors—mom and daughter. However, the mother does not want to let go; she maneuvers to impede maturity. The proper boundaries are not established, and normal bonding is thus interfered with.

This type of mothering intrudes in the friendships and communications of the growing girl. The girl's private space may be invaded without notice. There are prying questions. The narcissistic engulfing mother also tends to project her own preferences on the daughter, claiming that she really likes this or that type of food or fashion or whatever, rather than the one that the daughter says she likes.

Another negative mothering behavior on the part of the narcissistic-smothered woman is meddling in the daughter's relationships. Typically, she puts down a close friend or husband or schemes to make them unhappy with a view to disrupting a good relationship. She does this out of envy and resentment.

From this behavior mentioned above, the daughter feels pressure not to assert herself and her own tastes and choices. She may not readily stand up to the mother because of the perceived associated risks of anger on the part of the mother or unfair criticisms and other demonstrations of rejection. Should the daughter demand to distance themselves, the mother will persist nonetheless. It could lead to actual stalking and other forms of harassment.

The engulfing type often idealizes her girl in the extreme. Sometimes the daughter is always the reason for the mom's problems and shortcomings. In other cases, she is just plain cold and negligent, absorbed as she is in her own self-admiration and selfishness. Her tactics vary, corresponding to each of these three styles.

To the engulfing mom, there is only the mother. There is no daughter, from her perspective, so the mother assigns herself the right to control and intrude. She may engage in asserting her right as a mother while treating the grown daughter as a little child. She may seek to disturb the balance between relationships by coming between a third person and the daughter (i.e., triangulation).

Others may be fooled. Since the narcissist can be charming and alluring, even charismatic but certainly talkative in the interest of monopolizing the attention in any social circumstances, they may show admiration for the mother-daughter rapport they observe. It can appear to be an ideal relationship, one that is very close rather than pathologically domineering.

From Clinginess to Absence

Next, we proceed to the other end of the spectrum, the mother who ignores the daughter. This kind of mother is so self-absorbed that she has little time or thought for her daughter. Naturally, the impact is quite painful and confusing.

The mother may be physically present most of the time but does not engage with the daughter. She remains withdrawn from the relationship with the daughter and preoccupied with herself and her own activities or ideas. Approaches may only achieve annoyance from this mother. She does not want to listen. She is negligent about the normal duties of parenting: from personal grooming and hygiene, counseling about life, to household organization.

Attempts to raise issues or inquire as to why the mother is so distant get few responses. The reply is more likely to be the cold shoulder or some pretext to move away and refrain from conversation. The reader can well imagine the lack of affection in these circumstances. Any hugging may only be mechanical and tentative on the part of the mother who likes to ignore the child. There are no questions about how the school is going or how the girl is feeling, etc. There are never any compliments. No encouragements. Any conversation likely is conducted with an arrogant or condescending tone.

As the child grows up and carries on her life, there are no phone calls or invitations. Any recognition of a birthday or some other special occasion such as a graduation is addressed nominally, superficially. If any gifts appear, they are according to the mother's own tastes and pushed forward as if the daughter may not be intelligent enough to see its value and suitability, even if the gift is not at all relevant or likable to the younger woman.

Unlike the clingy relationship of the smothering mother, the engulfing, it is easy to remove oneself from the company or attention of the ignoring mom.

Regardless, the pain of the emotional and material neglect cuts deep. The daughter can feel unworthy in general as a result. She may not trust other people enough to build close relationships after the experience with this mother. She may feel she never belongs or is unlovable.

Precious Doll or Cause of All Trouble?

It is also important to be aware of the dual danger of the mothers who either imagine a Golden Girl who can do no wrong or the Problem Child who spoils everything. Should a narcissistic mother have two children, she may assign each one of these opposing roles in the family.

Projecting her internal idealization of herself, she exaggerates the attributes and accomplishments of the child she sees as golden. She sits on a privileged and beautiful pedestal above others. This one can never do anything wrong, in her eyes. Any bad behavior or weakness is dismissed while any success or positive feature, no matter how small, is elevated. The narcissistic parent of this one will shower this family member with rewards and support, such as money for clothes, lessons, trips, etc.

Conversely, the scapegoat child is branded the black sheep. All problems of the family, especially those of the mother, are supposedly because of her. This one is placed low on the totem pole, in a dark corner to be spat upon and cursed. Any achievement or positive attribute is squelched or ignored. She is unattractive or even ugly, socially inept, academically stunted, physically repulsive, and so on and so on. She is not worth investing any support in at all.

Should there really be two children forced into taking up opposing functions like this, they no doubt fight and compete. The golden girl has a license to criticize the scapegoat, but the scapegoat child can never win a battle or argument in this household. It is the scapegoat who likely will be punished should friction between them get out of control.

The narcissist certainly does not want to accept that the child labeled the scapegoat is right about anything; nor does she wish to find fault about anything to do with the child given the golden role. Doing either would lead to the narcissist to discover her own weaknesses and mistakes. She does not want to recognize the achievements of the scapegoat child; in fact, that child may be rewarded for failure (e.g., receiving hugs or gifts as signs of love only when something goes wrong).

Indeed, she may be conceived of having something wrong with her, being sick in some way. On the other hand, no recognition of any fault or problem with the golden girl will be made. Her achievements are inflated and over-compensated. She is a healthy one doing well, always. Therefore, the one that is seen as the problem child probably will develop some medical issue such as an eating disorder or depression. The neuroses of the opposite figure are different—perhaps blossoming into a narcissist herself but certainly having anxiety about living up to perfection. There could be other bad habits such as deceit and manipulation so as to help the narcissist mother keep up the façade.

Perhaps, the scapegoat child is the one with the greatest

advantage, in the end, however. That's because neglect can drive her to become independent while the smothered child may never be free of the mother's domination, idealization, and control. The latter will have less baggage than the former.

Fathers Who Enable the Narcissistic Mother

What about the narcissistic mother's partner who is the father figure for the daughter? How does he respond? What's his parenting style in the face of his narcissistic spouse?

Unfortunately, in most instances, chances are, he is an enabler. If not the enabler, he probably shares the disorder or has taken off. Should he wish to stick around, how? He would have to support the narcissism.

The father in this type of scenario may be dysfunctional if he too is narcissistic. If he is not, however narcissistic, it is likely that he worships his wife, no matter what, otherwise, the father who is physically present plays along with the defensive narcissistic mom. Out of fear, he adopts the position of the sidekick to echo and assist. He becomes passive and lets the narcissism play out, despite the harm to the daughter, himself, and the woman.

He may become the guy who does the dirty work of attacking the daughter so that the mother can always appear correct, the enforcer deployed to either keep the daughter subjugated to the mother or prevent rebellion. He may rationalize the mother's wrong words and actions. If his partner gets angry, he follows suit or defends her with even greater rage. He may accuse the daughter of being a problem, endeavoring to make her feel ashamed or guilty, should she protest her treatment and desire her freedom and respect.

In most instances, the relationship between the narcissistic mother and the father is one of co-dependency, not love. The father may be anxious about maintaining the structure imposed by the mother and fear change or instability, so he entrenches himself in the accepting attitude and sets himself up as the prop onto which his leading star can lean.

Bloodsucking

The narcissistic woman, with her inflated sense of self and hypersensitivity to problems and criticism, may thrive on drama. The ignoring narcissist tends to make a big deal of the events in their lives and the effects on their emotional state while paying no heed to or suppressing the daughter's ups and downs. This parent is not interested in the disappointments, joys and exciting episodes of her own daughter's life; rather she makes the most of her own.

Everything is supposed to revolve around her. She may even dramatize the experience of others—neighbors, other family members, co-workers or business associates—so as to counter-pose them to her child's experience and try to make her child's life seem smaller. The smothering mother may tell the daughter she is just being a baby when the daughter mentions some trouble or goes through a defeat or disappointment. She may use the daughter's experience to underline the necessity of the daughter remaining under the wing of the engulfing mother, turning it into a justification for not spreading her wings to venture outside of the relationship.

Narcissistic mothers are like a vampire because they prey on the suffering of other people around them. She might display pleasure at passing on bad news for her child. She may exaggerate the misfortunes of others and their consequences and attach causes such as a person (here the child's) inabilities, unluckiness or deficiencies. Think of it—a miscarriage, a break-up, a rejection from a study program—the mother blames the daughter for these saddening and unfortunate events. This parent would most certainly deny any responsibility were there any that lead to disappointment.

Even at a funeral, the narcissist wants to make herself the focus of attention. She interprets what is happening as being related to her. For example, she may imagine that she was specially invited to attend because of her importance, not out of a duty to pay respect and express condolences. She may go on about how drastically the death hit her, not the tragedy it may mean for the deceased person and their loved ones.

Accusations that this woman is thriving on the tragedies of others would be stymied. They would hit a brick wall. Well, denial is a hallmark of many disorders, no?

Chapter 5
The Signs That You Have a Narcissistic Mother

> **THOSE WHO SAY IT COSTS NOTHING TO BE KIND, HAVEN'T MET A NARCISSIST.**

It is sometimes hard to know when we are dealing with a narcissist or not. They are going to be found amongst us, but figuring out the difference between someone who is maybe just a bit of a jerk, someone with a good sense of confidence, and someone who is a narcissist can be difficult. There are a number of symptoms and behaviors that you need to look for in order to determine if you are dealing with someone who is a narcissist or not. Some of the signs that you can watch out for include:

A sense of entitlement and superiority

When the narcissist looks at the world, they see that it is in black and white. Everything is either good or bad, right or wrong, and there is no in-between. With the narcissist, there is a hierarchy in the world, and the narcissist likes to put themselves right at the top. This is really the only place where the narcissist is going to feel like they are safe. The narcissists, at least in their own minds, have to be the best, the most competent, and the most right. Everything needs to be done their way, and they are the ones who have to be in control.

What is interesting here is that often, the narcissist is able to get the superior feeling that they want by being the worst out of the situation. They can be the most injured, the most upset, and the most ill for some time. This is done because it allows the narcissist to feel like they are entitled to receive concern from others, and it even allows them to hurt or demand apologies from others so that they can make things even.

A huge need for validation and attention

Narcissists are going to always need a lot of attention. They need it on a constant basis. These are the people who will follow their victim around the house, asking the other person to find things for them (even though they are perfectly capable of doing it on their own), and saying anything that is going to grab your attention. Even then, this doesn't seem to be enough for the narcissist.

When we look at the need for validation by the narcissist, it is like a funnel. You can pour in a lot of supportive and positive words; it seems like they just flow right through the narcissist and don't stick. You can spend all day telling the narcissist that you approve of them, admire them, and love them, and it is never going to be enough for them. Moreover, this is because most narcissists believe that deep down, no one can really love them. Despite their bragging and grand behavior, the narcissist is going to be insecure, and they have a big fear of not being able to measure up to others.

They need to be in control

Since narcissists are always going to be disappointed in the way that life unfolds around them, they are going to do what they can to try and control it, to see if they are able to mold it in some way to their liking

In the mind of the narcissist, there is going to be a story line about what each character in a specific interaction should be doing and saying. Of course, the real world doesn't follow this story line. and when that happens, the narcissist is going to feel upset about it. They will get mad and try to control the situation to their own liking.

They like to blame and deflect

Even though the narcissist is going to insist that they are the ones who are in control, they are never going to be responsible for any negative results. If the results of their control are good, they will jump right in and expect all of the praise and adoration that they think they deserve. However, if things don't fall into place or things don't go according to the plan that they had, then the narcissist will refuse to take the blame. There is always someone else to blame for the situation, and the narcissist will take advantage of this.

Sometimes the blame is going to be a bit more generalized. They may say things like all students, all bosses, all police and so on. Alternatively, the narcissist may pick one person to blame for the situation.

However, you may find that the narcissist is more likely to blame whoever is the most emotionally close to them, the one who is the most loving, loyal, and attached to them. In order to make sure that they always look perfect, the narcissist will always be able to find someone else to blame for things that go wrong.

Lack of boundaries

When it comes to knowing a narcissist, you may notice that they are not able to accurately see where they end and where another person begins. They think in a similar way to how a two-year-old would act, that everything belongs to them, that everyone else must feel and think the same way as they do, and that everyone, no matter who, wants the same things that they do.

What comes next is a lot of insult and shock when the narcissist finds out that someone is going to tell them no. If the narcissist wants to get something from another person, they are going to go through great lengths in order to figure out how to get it. They will use a lot of different techniques, including pouting, rejecting, demanding, cajoling, and persistence.

Lack of empathy

Narcissists are going to have very little ability when it comes to empathizing with others. They are going to be very self-involved and selfish, and they are going to run into trouble when it comes to an understanding of the way that others are going to feel. They think that everyone else is the same as them, and they don't really take the time to think about how others are going to feel. It is unlikely that you are going to find one who is truly guilty, remorseful, or apologetic in any way.

However, on the other end of things, the narcissist is going to be really attuned to any rejection, anger, and threat that they perceive from others. At the same time, they are going to be pretty much blind to the feelings of others around them. They can misread even the smallest of facial expressions, and they are going to be biased to thinking that all facial expressions are going to be negative. Moreover, unless you decide to act out these emotions in a theatrical manner, it is impossible for the narcissist to perceive what you are feeling.

Another issue that can come up is if your expressions and your words are not congruent, then the narcissist will respond erroneously. This is why it is common a narcissist is more likely to misinterpret sarcasm as an actual agreement or joking as a personal attack. Their lack of ability to read body language is one of the reasons that a narcissist is going to have trouble being empathetic to your feelings. They aren't going to see them, they aren't going to interpret the emotions right, and they pretty much assume that everyone else thinks the same way that they do.

Another thing to consider is that narcissists are going to lack an understanding of the nature of feelings. They don't really understand how or why feelings occur. They assume that feelings are going to happen outside of them, rather than something that is internal. They think that you are the one who causes their feelings, especially when it comes to the negative ones. They assume that because you aren't following along with their plan, or because they are feeling vulnerable around you, that you are the one to blame.

Emotional reasoning

It is likely that at some point, you have made the mistake of trying to use logic and reason with a narcissist in the hopes of trying to get them to understand the effect they are having on you. You think that if you talk about this, they will understand the way that this behavior is hurting you and that they will change. However, these kinds of explanations are not going to make much sense at all to the narcissist, because they are really only aware of their own feelings and thoughts. They may say that they understand up and down, but they really don't.

Because of this, narcissists are going to make decisions about how they feel about something. For example, if they like the way that they feel when they drive it, they will go out and have a red sports car. It doesn't matter if it is going to work in their budget or for their family.

Splitting

The personality of a narcissist is going to be split into both bad and good parts, and they are going to split up the things in their relationships as well. Any of the negative behaviors or thoughts that come up are going to be blamed on either the victim or other people. The narcissist is going to deny that they said any negative words, or did anything negative in terms of actions, while still accusing and disapproving of their partner. When they look back at things, they are going to remember them as either completely good or really horrible. There isn't a way for them to mix together these two things.

For example, have you ever gone on a vacation with someone who said that the whole thing was ruined because there was one bad day in terms of weather, or the reservation for the hotel vacation didn't meet their expectations? A narcissist isn't able to see, feel, or remember both the negative and the positive that came in the situation. They are able to just deal with one perspective at a time, and that perspective is going to be their own.

Anxiety

Another thing that you are going to notice with a lot of narcissists is that they are going to feel a lot of anxiety about what is going on in their lives. Some narcissists are going to show their anxiety by talking all the time about the doom that they think is about to happen, while there are others who are more likely to hide and then repress their anxiety.

For the most part, you will notice that a narcissist is going to project their anxiety onto the ones they love. They are willing to accuse the ones they love of being mentally ill, being unsupportive, of being negative, of being selfish, and of not responding to the needs of the narcissist. The reason that they do this is because it transfers some of the anxiety to the loved one, in the hopes that they, the narcissist, will not feel the pain at all. As the victim starts to feel worse and worse, the narcissist is able to make themselves feel better. In fact, this is a good way for the narcissist to start to feel stronger and like they are the superior one in the situation.

Shame

It is uncommon for a narcissist to feel a lot of guilt, simply because they think that they are the ones who are always right. Moreover, they don't have any idea that their behaviors are really having a negative effect on others. However, a narcissist is indeed going to feel a lot of shame. Shame, in this case, is going to be the belief that there is something either personally wrong or bad about who you are. Moreover, the narcissist is not going to like this at all.

Buried in a deep part of the narcissist, which they are going to repress quite a bit, are a bunch of insecurities, rejected traits, and fears. Moreover, the narcissist is going to keep these hidden so that others are not able to see them, even the narcissist. It is common for the narcissist to reject these feelings and thoughts because they are really ashamed of even feeling them at all.

Trouble communicating at work or inability to work as part of a team

Thoughtful and cooperative behaviors are going to require each person to understand the thoughts and feelings of another person. How is the other person going to feel when you act or say a certain thing? Will this action be one that is going to make you both happy? Is this action, or are these words going to make a change in your relationship?

These are questions that a normal person is going to ask when it comes to working with a team. But these are questions that a narcissist is going to have no motivation or capacity to think about. You should never expect that the narcissist is going to understand your feelings, they are not going to give up anything, and they will not give in just for the benefit of someone else. It will be useless to try.

Because of this, it is hard to work with a narcissist. They do not understand how others feel, and they have no want to learn how to do this either. So they are less likely to get along. They won't give in, they won't admit when they are wrong, but they will certainly take all of the credit when things start going well. They are really hard to work with and can make the whole team feel frustrated.

As you can see, a lot of the traits that come with being a narcissist are going to make it difficult for them to get along in society and do well. They are not able to understand the way that normal people are going to think, and they are much more interested in making sure that they are the ones who are in charge, and that they are the ones that get what they need. This can make it a challenge for them to get along well with others.

Then there could be an issue with parents who are too neglectful. This is going to cause the child to overcompensate, hiding all of the negative things that their parents didn't like about them when they were younger, and just trying to show off an image that is perfect to the world. Whether the neglect was intentional or not didn't matter, the individual may have learned how to just showcase their positive attributes as a way to make themselves look better and gain approval from the outside world.

Another cause that could bring out narcissism in an individual is if their parent, one or both, were narcissists. They would have learned this kind of behavior from their parent as they are growing up, and it is likely that they are going to exhibit the same kinds of personality traits as well.

Many people also worry about the connected world that we have right now. They worry that because the world is spending so much time on social media and online, rather than getting out there and making real connections with those around them, that narcissism is going to become a bigger problem in the future. People spend so much time alone without the help or interaction of others, and they spend so much time trying to show their best side online that it is no wonder that many of them are going to struggle when it comes to having narcissistic personality disorder.

Right now, many of the studies that have been done on this condition have not found a ton of therapies and treatments to help with this condition. Many times the narcissist doesn't see a problem, so they don't want to work on making that problem any better. Right now, the most common treatments to work with will be therapy, either group therapy or individual therapy.

If you have been around someone who has NPD and who is a narcissist, you will notice that they are going to have very little care for others. They are going to want to spend their time worrying about their own goals and needs, rather than the goals and needs of others. They have no empathy for others, and they assume that everyone else must feel and think in the same manner that they do.

These people feed on constant praise. Whether they are at work, at school, or in a relationship, they demand that the other person feeds into their need for love and attention all of the time. Also, they often need to be the best, the strongest, and the one who is the most right at all times.

When it comes to a relationship, this can be really harmful to the other partner. In order to keep the partner in place and to stay in that relationship, and to ensure that they are able to get a constant amount of love and attention, the narcissist is going to work to put their partner down. They will be the one in control, and the other person will feel like they have to depend and rely on the narcissist at all times.

When it comes to working, the narcissist is able to take control as well. They do well at being a boss because they do have a lot of the great characteristics that come with being the leader. However, they are also going to miss out on some of the ones that are needed as well. Narcissists like to be in control, but they will often take credit for all of the good things that happen in the business or with a project, even if they have nothing to do with it.

It is not uncommon for a narcissist to be the reason that a company starts to have some problems as well. The narcissist is not able to take any blame for anything that happens in the company. And they can never admit when they were the ones who were wrong. Because of this, they are going to keep going with poor decisions, and blaming other people, rather than taking care of the situation when it comes up.

Dealing with a narcissist can be hard. They refuse to admit when they are the ones who are wrong, and their main goal is to make themselves look good, and feed themselves a lot of attention and focus from others. And since they don't really understand the needs and wants of others, there comes an even bigger challenge to talk with them, to work with them, and many times being in a relationship, being related to them, and working with them can feel like a major headache to a lot of people.

Why do some people become a narcissist?

There are a lot of theories out there when it comes to why someone may be considered a narcissist. Many times those who are narcissistic turned out that way because they had parents who are narcissistic. In some cases, the child was neglected because the parents were busy, they got sick, or they were so focused on themselves (if they were a narcissist) that they were not able to pay attention to their child at all. But then there are times when the parents may have been too overindulgent and not able to let the child fail, or ever notice when something bad happened with that child. They only focused on the good.

Either way, the child was either told that they were all bad and they hid some of those bad traits about themselves, or they were all good, and they just won't admit that there are some negative traits that they should be aware of. This can lead to the narcissist hiding the bad, and only focusing on the good, exaggerating it to a point where they think that they are the best person around.

When you meet with someone who is a narcissist, you will notice that their levels of self-esteem are going to be inflated. They are going to be very fragile because of this, usually because the flip side of this self-aggrandized feeling leaves them with low self-esteem. So, because their self-esteem is so low, no matter how much others are going to praise them and try to bring them up, this person is going to react badly to any kind of criticism.

Being condescending is going to be another common dynamic that is found in a narcissistic relationship. Often this is a behavior that is going to be traced back to the need, a very desperate need, that narcissists have to be liked, adored, and above others.

Are there different types of narcissism to watch out for?

While it is common for all narcissists to show certain types of behaviors, you will realize quickly that not all of them are going to be the same. There are actually two broad types of narcissism that are recognized in our world today, including the vulnerable narcissism and the grandiose narcissism. These are going to be two different types of the same problem, and they are going to stem from different early childhood experiences and are going to lead to some different behaviors in a relationship.

Let's take a look at how each one is going to work. When you interact with a grandiose narcissist, you will notice that they show off a lot of dominance, aggression, and grandiosity. They are going to be less sensitive to what others say and usually a lot more confident in the process as well. You may find that these individuals are elitists, and they have no problem when it is time to tell everyone how great they are.

These narcissists want to be treated in this superior manner because they were treated that way as a child. And now that they are progressing through life, they still expect to get this kind of treatment from others. When we look at how this kind of behavior is going to influence a relationship, the grandiose narcissist is more likely to be unfaithful, and even to leave the other partner quickly if they feel that they are no longer getting that special treatment that they have come to know and expect.

Then there are the vulnerable narcissists. These individuals are going to be a bit more sensitive when we talk about emotions. They are going to have a kind of fragile grandiosity, where their narcissism is going to serve as a type of façade protecting some of their deeper feelings of incompetence and inadequacy.

You may find that these narcissists are going to go back and forth between feeling inferior and superior. They are going to feel like they are the victim most of the time, and they will be anxious any time that they think they are not getting the special treatment that they want.

When it comes to this kind of narcissism, it is going to

show up early in childhood, and it is a good way for the individual to deal with any of the neglect and the abuse that they had to deal with on a regular basis. When they are in a relationship, the narcissist is going to worry quite a bit about how their partners will perceive them. In addition, this kind of narcissist is going to be paranoid, jealous, and possessive about their partners and will not want those partners to leave their sight because of these issues.

Chapter 6
Treatment for Children of Narcissistic Mothers

> stop reconnecting with toxic people from your past because you're lonely. focus on getting better and attracting better

There are links between narcissistic parenting and the symptoms of self-blame and low self-esteem experienced and demonstrated by the children who have suffered narcissistic parenting. In 2004, Guile, Mbekou, and Lageix published the results of a clinical study of narcissistic youths and youths who had narcissistic parents. They were particularly interested in the responses of such parents and youths to therapy.

The study group consisted of 36 children from ages nine to 13. They were all in therapeutic programs with parental counseling and psychodynamic psychotherapy. They were assessed for narcissism and their attitude and use of psychology and social services.

The study revealed that children and parents assessed with narcissism were resistant to psychosocial services that offered treatment and support. They were less likely to take advantage of such treatment and support precisely because of narcissistic assumptions, biases, and emotionality. Child victims of narcissistic parenting tend to blame themselves and feel inferior, while the narcissistic child devalues other people, denies their issues, wants to avoid feeling vulnerable, and lacks motivation.

The Relevance of Self-Help

When it comes to moving past the issues created by a narcissistic mother, professional help is almost always recommended. Nevertheless, the individual could begin some mental processes to check their own problematic thoughts, emotions, and actions that arise from the effects of incorrect parenting. The main thing is to recognize that the parent has a mental health problem. Then she can identify some symptoms that the parent exhibits and narrow down the possible disorders.

It may well be that the parent suffers from more than one and also signals parallel conditions such as hypersexuality, anxiety issues, or substance abuse. Committed to researching what might be the ailments, the child of the narcissistic parent will come across narcissism and recognize it. Once she does, she can identify some of the symptoms of narcissism, which nurtures an understanding of the disorder.

There is no point in denial. Though a defense mechanism itself, denial blocks the path to the processes of understanding and committing to change the responses and the relationship. Neither is clinging to hope that the parent will love and take responsibility. This false hope is self-defeating.

This admission and acceptance may make it easier for the affected daughter to feel compassion for themselves and to gain comprehension of her own feelings, behaviors, and ideas. She can start to relate them to negative parenting. She can overcome anger at the parent for the lack of love when she sees that the parent has a serious problem, which is the parent's issue and not theirs — seeing the associations can empower the person and motivate them to seek assistance and make some changes. An important thing to understand is the lack of empathy. Also, it should be understood that this state of a person comes from a weak sense of self, lack of self-love and over-sensitivity or defensiveness on the part of the parent. The child of the narcissist may allow herself to detach from and reset the faulty relationship with the parent.

It is likely that the daughter of such a parent will be depressed. It will be important to recognize this and get treatment for depression. The person should come to understand that it is a normal response to abuse and lack of parental emotional nurturing. It is possible for the individual to understand, get over it, and move on in life. There is no point in attempting to fix it, and the past cannot be undone. As already stated above, the narcissist does not like to be challenged.

If there is a second parent present, concentrate energies and efforts in that direction. The child can be an enabler, assisting the second parent in asserting themselves, rejecting narcissistic behavior, and helping the parent to let go. The child can challenge the co-narcissist or narcissism enabler to become aware of their role and the effects it has had on the offspring. She can also stand up to and resist that parent's defense and justification for the narcissist. By winning him over to her side, a united front against the harmful parent can be established.

Furthermore, it is helpful for the child of a narcissist to know and appreciate the family roles and dynamics and her own place on the web. She can find out whether she falls into a category of golden girl or scapegoat. It can help foster understanding of the alienation from other family members and their own clinginess or dejection. It can make someone see how they may be serving narcissism or being manipulated and controlled by narcissism.

In addition, the person will have to draw boundaries. Aware of any behaviors that amount to fueling narcissism or being subjugated by it, the individual can begin to give up compliance and subservience. She can set up her own rules. Most importantly, she can learn to admit and act on her wants and feelings. She can adjust their identity and emotions. By this point, the process of renegotiating the relationship and separating oneself from narcissistic processes get hard. It takes quite a bit of time.

Understand your vulnerability and why narcissists may target someone. Identify other narcissists and stay away from them. Remove the stingers and needles they have assaulted you with. Do not let them contaminate and infect you. There is no need to blame oneself for what the parent is responsible for. Let go of blame and feel compassion for yourself and circumstances. Do not punish yourself anymore. Do not keep dragging yourself down. Get on with your own responsibility of living your own life and living with respect and dignity.

At the same time, it is important to acknowledge one's own feelings about the narcissistic parent. Do not judge. It is okay to feel compassion for the parent diagnosed with NPD. It is okay to reserve some love for that person. There could be ways of supporting the person if they admit to a problem and seek help. The child can be a catalyst for making treatment happen and keeping it up.

Explore the family history and understand the processes that have occurred and the roles and dynamics of the family led by a narcissist. Then, it is healthy to let oneself feel the pain from the bad experiences and the lack of nurturing. After that, gain some appreciation for signs of personal growth and life accomplishments despite the poor parenting and lack of familial support. The person should feel good about real assets and achievements.

Follow up that process by getting back out into the world on a quest to find new relationships or make relationships more functional wherever possible (probably not the relationship with the narcissist parent, but perhaps with siblings, the other parent and other relatives, friends, business and work associates). Overall, the efforts aimed at healing should be to arrive at a firmer and more confident sense of the self.

Next is the business of setting the boundary. The woman should let the mother know when she is intruding and violating her rights and duties as the mother of an adult. She should assert herself and stand up to the problem behavior that interferes and violates respect for her, no matter the antics and retaliations exhibited by that mother.

The main purpose is not to change the relationship with the mother (or narcissistic father); it is actually to change the relationship with the anxiety associated with the mother-daughter dynamic and the bad feelings it generates.

Therapy

Speaking of professional therapeutic options, the adult must first accept there is a problem, then look back at childhood and accept the reality of it. This takes abandoning fantasies about childhood. The person must be ready and equipped to be responsible for making a change. They have to account for the problem behavior and causal factors.

The five-stage therapeutic process of recovery includes the following. First is recalling and discussing experiences as a child. The childhood events are reconstrued in a more realistic way and the fantasies identified and rejected. Next, the person will feel sad about losing the fantasy because a way of thinking and behaving has been built around it. Also, the reality will no doubt be disappointing and sad. The foreseen benefit, however, is that the person no longer relies on hope based on the fantasies.

In the third phase, the narcissistic family and its symptoms and outcomes are appreciated and recognized. Considering herself in the present, the therapist and the client work together to sort out the positive thoughts, feelings, and behaviors from the negative ones, deciding which to keep and which to let go. The final stage necessary to pass through for recovery is making the commitment to change. The aim is to become more socially functional for success in areas of life, such as relationships, career, household organization, and inner happiness.

To clarify the process of initiating and carrying through with the change, it is necessary to articulate certain problematic behaviors that inhibit healthy functioning, starting with assertiveness. Because of the immersion in the life of a narcissistic family, the child growing up there may not know what they think and feel. There may be long buried sentiments. It will then be appropriate to learn communication skills especially to express feelings by means of certain techniques. The client thereby becomes more aware of what they think and feel and better skilled at conveying what they think and want. Functioning improves because the person can learn to say aloud what they prefer or expect or feel instead of walking away or getting angry.

Another area that needs work is by establishing boundaries. The offspring of narcissistic parenting may be reluctant to draw boundaries (between themselves and others, between their own likes and wants and those of others) because they do not wish to disappoint. Setting boundaries enables the person to take more control. Also, she learns to accept criticism and make it through disapproval.

Tips for defining boundaries include:

1. You are able to express your needs to others, although you cannot always get what you need from others.

2. How you feel is a reality. It is just what you feel and does not need to be rationalized.

3. Asserting your thoughts and feelings does not have to be destructive or hurtful. You can learn to articulate them effectively in an appropriate way.

Different experts offer different interpretations and recommendations for therapy and action to overcome the pain and correct poorly functioning thoughts and behaviors stemming from the experience of surviving a narcissistic parent. Most available treatments are for adults.

The chief issue with respect to therapy is self-worth and self-respect. This devaluation of the self may even be a result of rejecting narcissistic behavior and an effort to avoid behaving like a narcissistic person. They counter the fear of developing narcissism by under-valuing themselves.

To improve self-esteem, the offspring of the narcissistic parent will have to retrace the history of their childhood. The parents probably will not offer any help. In fact, they could be a hindrance to the process by reconstructing the past to suit them. Part of the reason is their own condition of coldness and self-centeredness. That is precisely why intervention by a professional therapist is vital.

The client will probably need to shed any belief that the narcissistic parent has empathy and is interested in correcting things. She will not likely accept the revised version of the past and the truth of the relationship with her. Compassion for oneself and distance from the parenting is bound to aid the person to recover. It is possible that big results can happen through professional therapy for the person who has suffered under the shadow of a narcissistic parent.

Cognitive Behavioral Therapy (CBT)

Cognitive Behavioral Therapy (CBT) is a type of therapy that focuses on analyzing why a person feels the way they do based on the unique ways they view specific scenarios. As a variety of mental health issues are based on distorted ways of looking at the world, CBT is effective because it shows patients the error of their thoughts.

Cognitive Behavioural Therapy functions around a handful of core beliefs, starting with the fact that thoughts lead directly to actions and can also influence behaviors. This is usually represented on a diagram in a cycle. It illustrates that if we can change one component of the cycle, then we can change all three. It also shows how these things are all interconnected rather than independent of each other.

The second concept is especially important as it relates to anxiety (even though CBT can treat many forms of mental illness). Anxiety's non-stop obsession with what can be makes us feel like we've lost control over our lives and everything around us. However, that isn't the problem. The problem is that it tries to make us take control of everything to protect ourselves. CBT teaches us to accept what's beyond our control and to recognize and hold on to what is. This is largely done through introspection.

CBT works on the assumption that thoughts, behaviors, and feelings are all constantly interacting and influencing each other. Thus, the way a person thinks or interprets a given situation will ultimately determine how they feel about it and thus, how they will react to it.

For example, consider a pair of individuals who both recently failed to do as well as they would like on a difficult and important test. The first person thinks that if they were smarter, they would have done better on the test, which must mean that they are stupid. They feel anxious about the idea of future tests and depressed about their prospects for the class overall. As a result, they develop a negative opinion of themselves while at the same time not taking any positive actions when it comes to improving how they prepare for future tests as they now believe that their lack of basic intelligence is the root of the problem.

The other person, on the contrary, decides that the only reason they did poorly on the test was that they didn't study enough as they thought they already knew the material. While this will lead to feelings of disappointment in the short-term, it will also make it possible for them to feel better about the next test they have. What's more, it also leads to more productive behavior in the future as they can more readily ensure that the same thing doesn't happen next time by studying more thoroughly in the future.

What really distinguishes Cognitive Behavioural Therapy apart from the other kinds of therapies is the fact that it is structured around completing two separate, distinct tasks, which are Cognitive Restructuring and Behavioral Activation.

Cognitive Behavioural Therapy also places most of its focus on the present by bringing out the way the patient feels in the moment rather than the underlying reasons the patient might feel a specific way.

Cognitive Behavioural Therapy is also known for its focus on specific problems the patient might be facing rather than the more general picture of all issues or the patient's overall mental state.

In either group or individual sessions of the CBT, problem thinking and behavior will be identified first, then prioritized and then finally addressed in order of necessity.

CBT is primarily education-based, which means that the therapist is going to use structured learning experiences as a way for patients to learn to monitor the negative thoughts and images that come into their minds. The goal, then, is to recognize how these contradictory ideas affect the physical condition and behavior and to understand how these things affect mood.

It is also important to note that CBT patients are generally expected to take an active role in their therapy experience as well. This means they are going to be regularly given homework assignments after each therapy session, some of which will even be graded.

These assignments will be reviewed at the beginning of each session. During sessions, a wide variety of different strategies are going to be used, including things like behavioral experiments, guided discovery, imagery, role-playing, Socratic questioning, and more. Despite this, CBT sessions are typically limited in nature, rarely lasting more than four months.

While each of the exercises discussed in the following chapters is going to be more effective for treating some issues than others, this doesn't necessarily mean you are going to find something to deal with your specific issues here.

To determine if Cognitive Behavioural Therapy is a good fit for you, there are some questions you can ask yourself:

Do you prefer focusing on your current problems as opposed to those from the past?

Do you believe that talking about your current troubles is more useful than discussing childhood experiences?

Do you consider yourself to be primarily focused on achieving your goals in as short of a period as possible?

Do you prefer therapy sessions where the therapist is active instead of just a passive recipient?

Do you prefer structured therapy sessions over those that are open-ended?

Do you feel willing to put in effort on your own to support your therapy?

If you answered yes to a majority of these questions,

then CBT is likely going to be effective when it comes to helping you reach your goals. While there are some exercises you will be able to successfully complete by yourself; you will find that you are far more successful with the help of a professional as opposed to going it alone. Additionally, if you are dealing with any issues that may be life-threatening, it is recommended that you seek professional help as soon as possible to ensure you don't become a danger to yourself and others.

Neurological Relief

Eye Movement Desensitization and Reprocessing Therapy (EMDRT)

Brain scans can show patients the condition of the hippocampus (short-term memory bank at the rear of the brain). The hippocampus can be stimulated to regrow, and EMDR is a great place to start. Eye Movement Desensitization and Reprocessing Therapy (EMDRT) is one proven effective brain therapy. At least one research study indicates that the hippocampus of PTSD patients can grow back as much as six percent by the implementation of EMDR. This technique works on soothing the excessive stimulation of the amygdala, the center of basic emotions such as fear.

EMDRT results tend to be visible fairly quickly with over 30 controlled studies in the past decade finding that victims of a single trauma were able to see measurable improvements after 270 minutes of treatment spread out across three sessions. This efficacy is improved to 100 percent among single-trauma cases and 70 percent in multi-trauma scenarios when treatment is instead spread out over six sessions.

EMDRT works using a highly structured process that looks at not just the present but the past and future ramifications of stressful and negative memories as well. These steps are detailed below and should only be performed by those trained explicitly in EMDRT as it can do more harm than good when performed incorrectly.

EMDRT steps

1. Planning (Treatment and History): This step is relatively standard and includes an evaluation and a detailed history of the issue in question. Unlike some CBT variants, EMDRT is very interested in the client's past, specifically, distressing memories which are then tagged as targets of reprocessing. EMDRT is typically focused primarily on the most significant and most difficult experiences the client has been through as changing those will then cause the most noticeable change overall.

2. Learn to relax: An essential aspect of EMDRT is staying calm between sessions before learning to direct your eye movements yourself. Because of this, therapists suggest and help practice various relaxation techniques, including guided imagery before getting into actual EMDRT techniques. Another particularly useful relaxation technique that can aid in EMDRT is mindfulness meditation.

3. VOC Scale: The VOC scale, otherwise known as the Validity of Cognition scale is what is used to calibrate a person who is going to be using EMDRT for the first time. Initially, the patient will be asked to think of a specific image that you can relate negatively to,

before then doing the same thing with a positive image instead. The patient will then be asked to consider how completely they believe in the positive image, followed by the negative image. They will then be asked to list any feelings that the images might generate as well as their overall level of intensity. They will finally be asked to link those sensations with various parts of the body, if relevant.

4. Reprocessing: The reprocessing step of EMDRT focuses on retraining the brain to experience positive emotions as opposed to the negative ones that are currently associated with specific memories. As a part of this exercise, the client will focus on trouble spots for about a minute at a time. While doing so, they will also be asked to focus on something that will cause them to look either left or right, as opposed to in the way that is currently associated with the negative memory in question.

The nature of the added stimulus isn't important; what is important is that it remains in play long enough for the eye movement to be moved away from the trouble spot. During each session, the patient's eyes will be moved further and further from the trouble spot, improving their reaction to it in the process.

5. Improve beliefs: Once reprocessing has occurred a few times, the next step will be for the patient to retain the new patterns by relating back to the positive thoughts they generated earlier. This part of the process will also include another round of the stimulus from the previous step to ensure that future negative memories create the same mitigated response.

During this step, the patient must focus on each part of the new emotion, including how it makes them feel both mentally and physically. After they have a firm grasp on the emotion, they will then be instructed to think about it in conjunction with the stimuli in question with enough conviction that the two become interconnected in your mind.

Being mindful is a process of existing entirely at the moment using the information your senses are providing you as an anchor to prevent you from interacting with the thoughts that are racing through your head. The goal is to notice thoughts without interacting with them, and it can make avoiding negative thoughts before they lead to panic and anxiety easier than you may have ever thought possible. It can be practiced anywhere at any time, all you have to do is focus on breathing deeply and the physical sensations that doing so creates throughout your body.

The Treatment of Children suffering from NPD

A psychiatrist should talk to the child to examine how they see themselves. How much self-love and self-importance does she express? How is school going? Are there friends? A variety of assessment tools could be implemented. The doctor might decide to make use of forms such as questionnaires, and there may be tests according to scales.

When the therapist is introduced, the attitude displayed, and manner of interacting in response to the intervention is also looked at. There should be a full physical examination to determine whether other causes are at play.

Ruling out physical causes, psychoanalytic inquiry seeks to find out whether other disorders are presented. There could be depression, high anxiety or a coinciding second personality disorder.

Once it is determined the child has NPD, the extent of the disorder is measured. Is it mild, moderate, or severe? Is it based on moods only? Finally, a plan for caring for the mental health of the child is sketched out. Therapy may address recovery or, based on a diagnosis that the condition and its situation are highly complex; the goal may be the management of the disorder.

One kind or a range of cognitive behavior therapy (CBT) may be applied. This identifies problematic thoughts, emotions, and behaviors. Most schools of cognitive behavior therapy aim to stop these problems and eradicate or alter them, though the mindfulness and acceptance strain of therapies may aim at making the person aware of the negative inner processes and trying to have the client reset their values. The latter approach wants the client to under-value the negative personal experiences, assuming that they will remain in the background, by placing more value on healthy goals. The relationship to the negative experience is changed to redirect the person's life and help them function better.

Treating the Narcissistic Parent's Inner Child

The narcissist has, in all likelihood, built up a fortress to protect internal pain. The narcissist has her history with hurt and baggage, after all. She creates defense mechanisms to keep from feeling vulnerable or needy. The fear and vulnerability is the inner child.

There are a variety of emotions triggered by sensitivity the narcissist has trouble feeling as they are viewed as threats that could open up the inner pain. They are an aversion to ridicule, insecurity or lack of control, sensing deficiency, lack of emotional nourishment, and abandonment. The narcissist wants to prevent a release of their innermost true feelings and would prefer to keep up the charade. A therapist would perceive the denial or lack of insight about the person's real feelings and experiences; the emotionality would appear stymied or splintered. A big motivation is the covering up of shame for what lies beneath. The person could respond to therapy and learn self-compassion, understanding that it is okay to feel vulnerable. She could be encouraged to let the innermost feelings surface if there are accompanying tactics of self-soothing and a guiding, empathetic therapist.

This process can be successful if the therapist starts out by coaxing the inner child to reveal itself and developing a bond with that inner child. The therapist makes the therapeutic environment safe for the client. The therapist could operate as a role model, suggesting alternative emotional responses. A combination of psycho-education and role modeling can manage to get the client to accept and take on adjusted parenting behaviors and attitudes. This is done through a process of having the client re-parent herself and her wounded insides. Even if the client does not confess to any painful experiences, they could be led through the process anyway.

From there, a recovery plan could be constructed

wherein the basic, best parenting behaviors are identified in contrast with the non-functioning or harmful parenting behaviors. Stine characterizes this process as being akin to a treatment for addiction that needs to be mitigated and put aside. The adult learns to abstain from negative behaviors, including behaviors that are passive-aggressive responses, manipulating, blaming, entitling, womanizing, yelling, exiting dramatically, and substance abuse.

The client learns awareness of the need for self-protection and the strategies she uses to protect the inner child. Clients still get to protect themselves. They learn healthier ways of maintaining the self and shielding themselves from hurt and exposure. They learn healthier ways of responding to and interacting with others. In short, they correct themselves by learning how to care for themselves.

The therapist also has to take care of herself, because of the narcissist's tendencies to be abrasive, dependent and needy. Engagement with this type of client can be especially frustrating and draining. The therapist has to demand respect and maintain respect for the client but may need to take breaks and manage her own health during the program of therapy.

Chapter 7
Things Narcissistic Mothers Say for Mental Manipulation and Control

> Sometimes you need to stop seeing the good in people and start seeing what they show you...

To keep you under control, your mother has used different techniques that I'll describe later. Your mother may not have used all of them, and she may have used different techniques at the same time. Toxic mothers are quite predictable and have very similar action patterns. However, they are unique people, and not all use the same torture weapons. You'll recognize them as you read through them.

Reading the abuse techniques will bring you back to your childhood, to painful moments. Please keep your notebook with you. Each technique you read will take your memory to specific moments, stories that you may have buried.

Bringing them to memory again will hurt you. However, please write them down. Believe me, that the exercise of recognizing your pain, its origin, and taking it out will help you. Doing this is going to get you emotional, and will even bring out your emotional defensive behaviors like anger and great sadness. I recommend you that if you live with someone, partner, children, friends, share with them your healing process. You don't want them to worry about seeing you suffer.

But don't worry. I won't allow you to stay in pain. You'll see later that focusing on the pain leaves you chained to it. But to reach the part where you can start to change and heal. First you need to recognize what it's that you have. You need to be aware of every symptom you have.

Let's start seeing the abuse techniques that your mother has used to keep you under her control. Let your tears sprout; you need to clean yourself from pain.

Infantilizes

Infantilizing consists of underestimating physical and mental abilities, which favors a loss of independence and autonomy. This form of abuse translates into isolation and a diminution of the physical, cognitive, functional, and emotional faculties.

Examples of infantilization can be the following:

•   Give money constantly to the daughter, reinforcing the message that the daughter can't fend for herself. Logically, the daughter will never know how to survive and seek a life of her own if the mother doesn't let her.

•   Approve or disapprove of your friendships; she decides who is good or bad for you.

•   Telling you what you should wear.

- Saying you're too young to get married, to leave home, etc. (even if you're 40!)

- Write down how your mother infantilized you when you were younger and how she does it now. Take your time, read the point again if necessary. Go for a walk and let your memories come up.

Invalidation

Invalidating is rejecting, ignoring, ridiculing, mocking, judging or diminishing someone's feelings. The toxic mother controls how we feel and for how long we feel it. Does it sound familiar?

A child who is repeatedly invalidated, becomes a confused child and a toxic mother constantly invalidates you.

When you're invalidated as a child, and repeatedly told you are worthless, when you're older this is what you believe, and it's very difficult to reverse this feeling recorded in our being.

The invalidated, despised, humiliated, insulted child loses confidence in her feelings. She loses the use of her emotional brain—and the emotional brain is one of the necessary tools for survival.

Examples of invalidation that the toxic mother uses:

- Stop crying, or I'll hit you.
- I've done so much for you.
- You're not worth anything.
- Nobody is going to love you.
- Change your mood!

- Go screaming/crying somewhere else!
- What a bad character you have, nobody will want to be with you.
- You are already making a drama out of it.
- You don't fight enough.
- You are not responsible enough.
- Your room is a disaster.
- You look like a freak (although that day you are wearing your best clothes).
- You are very clumsy.
- I suppose you might be always wrong.
- You never listen.
- Get out.
- Shut up.
- Take it easy.
- It's already happened, it's not that bad.
- Don't bother me.
- You're overreacting.
- You cry for nonsense.
- You could have done better.
- You only give me problems.
- It's your fault
- Your examples. Write in your notebook examples of invalidation that your mother has used with you.

Gas lighting, emotional suffocation

This is one of the most destructive emotional abuse strategies. It's used by our toxic mothers to make us think we're sick in the head.

The toxic mother presents you with false information so that you doubt yourself, and even your sanity. Your mother convinces you that your way of seeing life is not true. So, if you've ever thought you are crazy, no, you're not. It was your mother who made you believe it.

Gaslighting is a form of psychological abuse that consists of presenting false information to make the victim doubt her memory, perception, or her sanity.

The abusive mother may make you wonder:

- Has it really happened?
- What has my mother really done?
- What has my mother said?
- Did I hear her properly?
- Have I not understood something?
- Wasn't I listening when she told me?
- Why do I always get confused?

Doesn't respect your personal boundaries

Personal boundaries are rules or limits that a person creates to identify what are the reasonable, safe and permissible ways for other people to behave around them and how they'll respond when someone steps on those limits. They are rules and principles you live by when you say what you will or won't do or allow.

They're constructed from a mixture of beliefs, opinions, attitudes, past experiences, and social learning.

Personal boundaries define you as an individual, delineating your likes and dislikes, and establishing the distances that you allow others to approach you. They include physical, mental, psychological, and spiritual limits, which include beliefs, emotions, intuitions, and self-esteem.

Personal boundaries are healthy and necessary in a person's life.

As the daughter of a toxic mother, you've been raised to have no limits. Nothing you own is yours, not even your body, certainly not your thoughts and beliefs. You aren't an individual person, separated from your mother; you are an extension of her. Unfortunately, that doesn't change when you're older, and it goes on even if you're 60 years old.

Your mother doesn't respect your physical, emotional, or psychological boundaries. She reads your letters, emails, or asks you exceedingly personal questions. You feel you have no privacy; she rummages in your closets, mail. She sets your time without asking you if it suits you.

One of the problems you have as a daughter of a toxic mother is that you've never been allowed to establish your own boundaries. Your mother has done it for you.

The problem of growing this way is that when you reach adulthood, you don't change: you don't know how to establish and enforce boundaries. So anyone can come and set them up for you: a boss, a couple, even your own children.

Let's see below the different types of boundaries that

your mother breaks.

Physical Boundaries

The toxic mother violates your physical space. She thinks she has rights over you, that's why she goes in while you're in the bathroom without asking, or she gets into a private conversation without anyone inviting her. If you move, she'll have the right to enter your home when and however she wants.

Mental Boundaries

Your mother invades your thoughts, opinions, and beliefs. Toxic mothers can't tolerate disagreement. So every time you've tried to express your own thoughts, she has reprimanded you, or worse, she's acted with anger and left you isolated, or ignored.

As a result, you've learned to live without expressing your own reality. Or if you've been the rebel, the scapegoat who has always continued to give her opinions despite knowing that you were going to be reprimanded, then you've always been labeled as the bad one, the cause of all the dysfunction and family problems.

The mental boundaries that your mother has imposed on you are the reason why you need constant approval from those you think are stronger than you. You doubt your thoughts and opinions. You need third parties to validate them.

Emotional Boundaries

The toxic mother limits your ability to have and control your own feelings.

She is only motivated by her wishes, and the people around her are there with the sole purpose of satisfying them.

The narcissistic mother tries to minimize the child's feelings if they are in direct conflict with her own needs. The child will be told that "she really doesn't feel that" or that she will "get over it" or "stop being a baby". She'll say or do anything that makes the child stop being so "dependent" because that requires that she puts her children before her own needs.

This has caused you to have grown up feeling that you're insignificant (your mother has ignored your feelings), and very hurt knowing that your mother has never cared about your true self. Moreover, worst of all, you've believed that your mother's feelings come before your own.

Have you written down all the boundaries your mother has broken with you? Write all the examples that come to your head. Make a list. Remember, she's broken not only the physical limits but also your emotional and mental boundaries. To how many things couldn't you say no?

Do you recognize the consequences of all these lacks of boundaries in your daily behaviors? Having not had intimacy, not having been able to express yourself as you would have liked to because you had to do things her own way, how did it make you feel? Write everything down, so that later you can work on it.

Practices triangulation

Triangulation is a sadistic manipulation method used

by a narcissistic person to manipulate two people while creating a triangle with her in the middle.

The triangulation in a dysfunctional family, with a toxic mother, basically consists of the mother competing the brothers and sisters against each other. This feeds envy, anger, and contempt, all highly corrosive emotions, to confront the siblings. Divide and conquer is something this emotional vampire understands.

The toxic mother is responsible for creating jealousy among siblings, through the unfair treatment of one of them (the scapegoat, the hated son/daughter or black sheep of the family) and of arbitrarily rewarding the other, (the golden child, the favorite and loved one). The toxic mother also triangulates through unfair comparisons created with the intention of disuniting the siblings.

Undermines your achievements

The toxic mother won't admit your achievements, except if she can attribute them to herself. Your mother will never let you be the one who appears as the one who does something right. She will attribute your success to her.

If the Sunday roast has gone well, it isn't on your own merits, but because you've used her recipe. If you get good grades, she'll tell everyone because it makes her look like a good mother. If she can't take credit for your achievements, she'll ignore them or despise them.

If you're going to be the center of an event, she won't be there, she'll be late, or she'll act as if it wasn't something so important. Alternatively, she'll make comments like "your brother's graduation was better." Or she'll try to make you feel bad before your big moment starts.

Uses a permissive father

A narcissistic mother can't act alone. She needs a permissive father. One who ends up being submissive to her or loves her to bits.

Within a distorted family with a toxic mother, there is always a permissive father. That father who actively or passively allows the mother to perpetuate her emotional terrorist acts.

So, as the daughter of a toxic mother, you feel like an orphan. Not only have you lacked an affectionate mother, but your father is also like he hadn't been present.

Practices projection

Projection is a dysfunctional tool that the toxic mother uses to put up with her shortcomings and limitations. She projects in you what she is, or what she's jealous of in you. When a toxic mother accuses you of lying, of being unstable, selfish, a bad person...she's accusing you of what she is, she's projecting herself onto you.

To understand it better we'll see what the projection is:

It is a defense mechanism by which the person attributes to other people their defects, thoughts, and even their shortcomings. It's a blame-shifting.

Your mother denies her own qualities and attributes them to you.

Projection can be divided into:

Neurotic projection is about perceiving others in ways that we unconsciously consider criticizable in ourselves. It is when people attribute feelings, attitudes, or motives, they find unacceptable in themselves, to someone else.

It ignores her problem and attributes it to you. It gets rid of that internal load and leaves it outside.

Deflection

Deflection is the art of psychologically and emotionally distracting a person from changing the subject, and focusing the conversation elsewhere. Your mother is the queen of deflection, she practices it so well, that when you're having a conversation with her, you probably end up scratching your head because you don't know what she's talking about.

It's a conversational control method. Clear, simple, and very effective.

Mothers with narcissistic personality disorder are artists of deflection. It's one of their favorite tactics to confuse your mind and make you doubt.

Intimidation. She generates fear.

Intimidation is an act that tries to generate fear in another person so that they do whatever you want. Normally the person who resorts to these tactics doesn't usually use aggression and violence, at least not in an obvious way because their main objective is to manipulate their victim without damaging their image.

It's easy to notice what the abusive person wants because her speech is plagued by indirect threats, which are implicit in her words. She makes it clear to her victim what the consequences of her actions would be and that the responsibility is solely hers. For example, your mum can say: "it's up to you, but I've already told you that you won't do it well", "if you don't do this, I won't buy you new pants."

Blaming to make you feel guilty

Blaming a person is a form of psychological abuse. Some psychologists define it as emotional manipulation.

People who blame know how to make you feel bad. They use guilt to manipulate you to do what they want.

Guilt can be transmitted with words, tone of voice, or even a look. The blamer likes to play dirty. To get away with what she wants, your mother takes advantage of your desire to please her and be a good person.

If your mother is trying to make you feel guilty, part of her behavior may be motivated by her own feelings of guilt that she's not recognized or resolved.

Munchhausen. Syndrome by Proxy.

This actually isn't an abuse technique, but a disorder that your toxic mother can have. However, I've included it in this section because it's a disorder that consists of making children sick, which is a form of abuse.

Munchausen Syndrome by proxy is a disorder in which a person, usually the caregiver or mother of the child, deliberately causes injury, illness, or disorder to another person, usually the child. It's a psychiatric disorder registered in the DSM-V as Factitious, or artificial, disorder.

It's a form of child abuse in which one of the parents causes in the child real or apparent symptoms of a disease.

There are cases in which mothers with a narcissistic personality disorder make their children sick to keep them under their power and thus obtain their narcissistic supply. Sicking their children gratifies their psychological needs for care and dependence.

The Silence Treatment

It is a set of behaviors that aim to ignore the other person. It's a form of covert psychological abuse. An attempt to control and vex others. It constitutes a harmful and toxic behavior that can cause diverse and serious effects in the other person.

Rejection

The toxic mother usually shows a rejection behavior towards the "bad daughter" or scapegoat. She lets you know in a variety of ways, you aren't wanted.

Leaving aside a child's value or belittling their needs is one of the ways of how emotional rejection can happen. Other examples of rejection may include telling a child to leave, insulting him or telling him that he's worthless. The mother will always blame the family problems on the child that becomes the scapegoat of the family.

Other examples of rejection from a mother to her

children are:

- Constant criticism.
- Abuse.
- Telling the child that he/she is ugly, or messing with his/her physical appearance.
- Shout or curse directed at the child.
- Frequent disparagement and use of labels like "stupid" or "idiot."
- Constant degrading jokes.
- Verbal humiliation
- Constant teasing about the body type of the child.
- Rejecting hugs and affectionate gestures.
- Excluding the child from family activities.
- Expressing regret about the child's sex or even that he/she was not born.
- Expelling the child from the family.
- Your own examples. What forms of rejection have you experienced? In which ways has your mother made you feel like you were not part of the family? Write on your notebook everything that comes to your mind.

Exploitation and physical violence

Exploitation can be considered manipulation, as it is the act of using a minor for personal advantage. A narcissistic mother takes advantage of her children in different ways.

Giving a child responsibilities that are much greater than those of a child's age is exploitation. Using a child for profit is abusive and is also another act of exploitation.

Although most mothers with narcissistic personality disorder are quite well disguised, and their "tortures" aren't visible for people outside the family, there are some that use more easily detectable methods.

Some of the habitual acts of exploitation for a narcissistic mother are:

A child who becomes a "caretaker" of his mother.

Making the child feel she is expected to take care of the other younger siblings.

Blaming a child for the bad behavior of the other siblings.

Giving unreasonable responsibilities to a child.

Encouraging participation in pornography.

Allowing her children to be sexually abused by partners or family members.

Perspecticide, brainwashing

One of the most dangerous manipulation techniques is to change the victim's way of perceiving herself.

The word "perspecticide" has been used to refer to the brainwashing to which prisoners of war were subjected, and its use is spreading in psychology to refer to the brainwashing of a person abusing his/her victim.

The objective of the perspecticide is to achieve a total loss of identity in the victim. The toxic mother doesn't want you to think for yourself; she'll try to erase your identity.

Perspecticide always implies an abusive relationship, control and manipulation, so that over time, the narcissistic person changes her victim's way of thinking.

Your narcissistic mother ends up defining your world. She defines what love is for you, how you handle your relationships and even how you should think or dress.

Some examples are:

Deciding how the victims should invest their time.

Obsessive control over everyday detail.

Change of self-concept. The narcissistic person makes sure to "steal" the victim's self-concept, placing her own in its place. This way, the perception of the victim changes, who begins to see herself with the eyes of the other person.

The person with narcissistic personality disorder decides on her victim, how she has to dress, what kind of work she takes, and how she has to behave.

Cognitive empathy

I know that you've always heard that narcissists don't have empathy. However, empathy can be good or bad.

According to the dictionary, empathy is defined as: 'the ability to understand and share the feelings of another.'

The definition doesn't mention anything about experiencing compassion, remorse, or humanity.

There are different types of empathy:

- Emotional empathy occurs when you feel the same

pain of those around you even if you are not experiencing pain. (You cry when your friend's dog has died)

• Compassionate empathy: you understand a person's difficulties, but, as you aren't experiencing them, you can act and help to improve the situation.

• Cognitive empathy: you perceive and understand the emotions of another. Cognitive empathy implies having a piece of more complete and accurate knowledge about the contents of another person's mind, including how the person feels. Cognitive empathy is more of a skill and you can train and develop it. It's a well-developed ability in skilled marketers and many lawyers who use it to get what they want. Moreover, of course, it's a skill that the narcissist excels at.

Compartmentalization

According to Wikipedia compartmentalization is "An unconscious psychological defense mechanism used to avoid cognitive dissonance or mental discomfort and anxiety caused by a person who has values, cognitions, emotions, beliefs, etc. in conflict with each other. Compartmentalization allows these conflicting ideas to coexist, inhibiting direct or explicit recognition and interaction between separate compartmentalized ego states."

In summary and applied to the narcissistic mother, she changes her entire focus to a situation in question and suppresses the feelings that usually accompany it (a popular example of compartmentalization is that of soldiers on the battlefield who put aside any guilt associated with killing people when they are in combat.)

Hoovering, she tries to suck you back

When your mother feels your distance from her, and she loses control over you, she tries to suck you back into the cage. She doesn't do it because she is repentant, or because she loves you, but because she needs to control you to inflate her ego.

Your mother will use your emotional weaknesses to bring you back. (She blackmails you emotionally by making you feel bad so you come back). As you will see later when you begin to see the aftermath that the abuse has left you, you try to get apart from her, but at that moment she gives you something good to attract you back. Manipulating you emotionally, she creates a traumatic bond with you that keeps you close to her.

Victimization

When all the manipulation tactics we've seen fail, your mother resorts to victimhood. She passes all the responsibility to you and resorts to emotional blackmail, pretending to be the victim of the situation. She victimizes to the point that you end up feeling bad for your behavior, when in fact you haven't done anything wrong.

Being "the victim" your mother, the abuser, generates a feeling of guilt in you that keeps you trapped in her net.

The empathy that characterizes you makes you fall into her trap and, by becoming the "bad guy" of the movie, you're more inclined to give in to her demands—this way she manipulates you without you being aware of it.

Revenge or harassment

If your toxic mother can't change you or make you return with her, then she'll change how others see you. Revenge. It looks like it, and it is.

The abuser can't bear to be abandoned, and that's when she loses her mind and tries to torment you.

She'll try to attack you socially, morally, and physically. Any way to hurt you is valid. Her ego is so hurt that she only seeks revenge.

When you separate from your mother because you see everything she's done to you, you expect her to react and somehow show some tenderness, some maternal instinct. Nothing could be further away from the truth. Like any other person with a narcissistic personality disorder, when you leave her, she'll try to hurt you as much as she can.

Chapter 8
Protection Tips

narcissist filter: what they accuse others of is actually an unconscious admission of their own character

Many people think that schizophrenia, stress, anxiety, and depression are the only kinds of mental health problems, but the list is a lot longer. Eating disorders, borderline personality disorder, bipolar disorder are all mental health problems.

Personality disorders are just a subcategory of mental health problems. People who have these disorders have unhealthy thinking and thought patterns. They will have behavioral problems, too. These thinking patterns are very rigid, and it takes much therapy to change and challenge these patterns with time. Many people who have this disorder will have problems perceiving and relating to situations and people.

Causes of NPD

Nobody really knows what causes NPD. It isn't easy to ask what causes mental health problems like depression. Some people are more susceptible than others. With NPD, some have it while others don't. Some will have a little; others will have an extreme case. It is a mystery, but studies suggest that the following problems might be some risk factors that can cause NPD later in life:

- Unrealistic expectations.
- Hereditary problems like oversensitivity and genes.
- Trauma early in life.
- Negative experiences in childhood like poor parenting or abuse.
- Experienced a lot of criticism.
- Psychological problems.

Narcissists are made. They aren't born that way. While genes do play a part, it is thought that experiences have more influence on developing NPD. It won't happen overnight but can happen at any age. It mostly happens during childhood because of poor parenting like over praising, over-pampering, being insensitive or from negative experiences.

Diagnostic Criteria

Diagnosis of narcissism is hard, and since most people who have this problem don't look for help, most doctors don't have a lot of experience in diagnosing the condition. Most doctors will refer the person to a mental health professional. In order for them to be diagnosed properly with NPD, they will have to meet five or more of the following:

- Being arrogant regularly.
- Having an exaggerated sense of self-importance.
- Believing others are jealous of them.
- Needing excessive admiration and compliments.
- Being jealous of others.
- Extreme sense of entitlement.
- Lack of empathy.
- Exploits and takes advantage of others.

Thoughts and Actions of Narcissists

Trying to get into a narcissist's mind is hard to do. Everyone acts and thinks differently, and each person is unique in the way they react and approach situations. A narcissist has a set behavioral pattern, and this makes them stand out. While there might be some anomalies in place since everybody is different, there are two examples:

- Using Covert or Overt Methods

For a narcissist to manipulate a situation or person so their needs are met, they might use methods that are described as either overt or covert. Overt is very obvious, where covert methods are very secretive and slide under the radar. Covert methods are very destructive to others, and this is why people who are in a relationship with a narcissist have problems leaving. They begin to questions whether it is them or me. A classic method is gaslighting.

A normal narcissist will always use overt methods. A vulnerable narcissist is going to use covert methods. A malignant or toxic narcissist is going to use a mixture of both.

- Cerebral or Somatic Approach

This is talking about the way a narcissist appreciates themselves and things. A narcissist who uses somatic methods will be totally taken with how they look, their general appearance, and their body. They are extremely vain. The cerebral method is using their brain, and seeming to be very intelligent. This narcissist will take great lengths to convince others that their opinion is needed and the only one that matters.

It is important to identify the type of narcissist that you are dealing with. While it could be hard to pinpoint exactly, you should be able to identify the dangerous type. A malignant or toxic narcissist won't have any problem hurting other people and won't show any remorse. This narcissist damages everybody around them. Anybody who is lucky enough to get out of a relationship with this type of narcissist is going to need a lot of emotional support or therapy after.

You may be reading this and wondering how anybody can't see there are things wrong with how they are thinking and acting. This is exactly how NPD works. You have to remember that narcissism is a personality disorder, and this creates a warped way of thinking. Narcissists will completely 100 percent think that you are wrong, and you should see their uniqueness. You shouldn't argue with them since they are always right. They will never look at themselves and think that they might be wrong. They might think that they would have handled the situation differently and better. True narcissists don't see a problem with how they act or think. When dealing with a malignant or toxic narcissist, these people don't see a problem with hurting others for their own gain.

Why A Narcissist Won't Get Treated

Many narcissists won't realize that there is a problem. If somebody tells them they should seek help since they are showing narcissistic behaviors, they will laugh or turn it around on you.

This isn't true for everybody. If a person has a mild form of narcissism, there could be an "aha" moment where they might think: "hey, I wonder if this applies to me?" when they are reading about narcissism or if somebody points out they are showing narcissistic behaviors. This is extremely rare and it is unlikely that a vulnerable or classic narcissist will ever seek help.

Will they get help? With some, they will but only after they have self-destructed or hurt someone close to them very badly. If a moment pushes them to a point, it might be that medical help might be accepted. In spite of all that, it is still unlikely, and it is a very sad fact.

Will Treatment Help?

There are various treatments for narcissism, but many centers around challenging thought patterns and behavioral changes. In extreme cases, it might be recommended that they are hospitalized, especially for extreme narcissists who have become very self-destructive.

The biggest problem is that treatment centers focus around solving the incident instead of solving the condition.

Can treatment help? It could, if they seek help, but it will take a lot of commitment and effort on the narcissist's part. Treatment isn't easy, and this goes for any type of problem that requires challenging thoughts and mindsets along with cognitive behavioral therapy. This treatment method won't be successful overnight and is going to require a long time along with maintenance treatment after that.

Personality Disorders Like Narcissism

Many mental health problems and personality disorders are linked together in some way. A person that suffers from depression could also have anxiety. A person who has stress could also suffer from anxiety. A person who has been diagnosed with bipolar disorder might have narcissistic behaviors. A person who has been diagnosed with a borderline personality disorder might have NPD, too.

In spite of all of that, there are three personality disorder that link closely to NPD:

- Histrionic personality disorder
- Antisocial personality disorder
- Borderline personality disorder

A healthcare professional can assess if a certain type of disorder is there, but talking someone into seeking help is hard, especially if they have narcissism.

Dealing with the Abuser

Now that you have decided to cut ties with your narcissist, you might be wondering if it is fine to remain friends with this person? In specific cases, it could be impossible to totally shut the door on your abuser even if you want to. Immediate family, friends, and coworkers that you have to see constantly will have a presence in your life.

Can you still be nice to them? The answer is no and yes. First, nobody expects you to "clean things up" with your abuser. If you feel that remaining civil would work best, them it could work out. While we are on the topic of being civil, is it possible to be civil to a narcissist. It is questionable if they can understand or adapt to that.

Resuming a relationship after a fight with a narcissist will take repentance and an apology from the offender, and, remember that a narcissist won't ever take the blame for anything, even if you know they did it. Without apologizing, the narcissist won't even think about being civil.

What does this mean for you? Simply that trying to have a "civil" relationship may be one-sided. Unfortunately, your abuser might take this opportunity to embarrass you if you try to initiate contact.

You could try to reach out and talk about the upcoming family reunion, but they might totally ignore or dismiss you once you begin talking. This is something they might do if there are other people around that see they are treating you with hatred.

Seeing as the narcissist has a pristine image with the other people who are around you, the people that see you being treated negatively will take the narcissist's side, that is if you did something wrong.

In many cases, the best thing to do after ending a relationship of any kind with a narcissist is to avoid them completely. Ignoring and treating them like a non-entity could be more beneficial for your emotional and mental healing. This will keep you from being drawn back into their trap. It also makes sure your abuse won't be able to exploit you.

Is it going to be easy? No. Most narcissistic abuse victims say the urge to reach out and talk or to ask forgiveness could pop up at any moment while you are healing from the abuse. This might even happen years after you have left the relationship.

Even though it may be hard, it isn't impossible. Try the following strategies to help you heal and strengthen your resolve to keep your distance from the abuser:

- Get Rid of All Communication

Block. Unfriend. Unfollow. This may sound harsh, but in this digital age, it is the worst thing you could do to somebody who is on social media. You also have to cut all ties that you have, or they could try to reach you in other ways to try and rekindle the relationship.

What if I really have to speak with them? Don't allow this thought to drive you to open ways of communication. What is important right now is you.

You have to keep your focus on recovering. Make sure not to leave any windows or doors open and don't allow any opportunities to let your internal mechanism push you into a conversation.

- Don't Update Your Life on Social Media

Nowadays, it's easy to find information on anybody's current activities and preoccupations. They don't call it the internet superhighway for no reason. The bad news is this could make it easier to keep checking on your abuser by getting tidbits of information on their life.

The biggest problem with stalking them online is it could spark flames. One flame is longing: the more you look at their updates and photos, the more you want to be back in their lives. The other flame is sadness: you see their life is going on without you, and the fact they aren't seemingly affected by your absence could injure your self-worth.

You need to remember that narcissists are masters of disguise. They are great at pretending. Your absence might have caused them some distress; they will make sure not to show you this. They are expecting you to look at their life. They have made sure to have images ready to hit you with.

- Think about the Truth

Even if you know you are right, you have a tendency to give other people the benefit of the doubt. This is just how reasonable people are. Even if you are dealing with an abuser, victims need to look at other angles. They might be hurting as well. They might have low self-esteem. They might be troubled.

Nobody other than you deserves your kindness and compassion. Narcissists aren't troubled people. They don't want to be fixed. They aren't acting out of trauma. This is the problem with narcissism. They don't "deserve" the compassion that most of us give to others.

Narcissists think they are better than others because they were brought up to believe they are. They fight to control everybody in their lives since they feel like they are entitled to power. They often think: "I am better than you, therefore you should listen to me so you can somehow achieve the same greatness." It is a completely toxic mentality.

Don't try to make sense of why they are acting the way they do. Try to think about the truth behind the actions. Yes, it is going to hurt at the beginning to see the behavior for what it really is, but make your mind see the truth, and it will be easier to keep your distance when they lose their luster and take on their true form in your mind.

- Stay Preoccupied

There isn't any strategy that is more effective that just keeping your abuser out of your mind. Your focus needs to be on you so do things that show yourself that you love yourself. When you constantly think about the painful abuse, it can be very negative if done to excess.

Take yourself out on a date, find a new hobby, and buy yourself something new. It will be better if you can find something you enjoy without needing anyone else's company. The more you can show yourself love, the faster you will find your self-worth. When that is in place, it will be easier to see the abuser for what they really are. This lets you detach yourself from your abuser further.

Chapter 9
Separating from a Narcissistic Mother

> Your life will get better when you realize it's better to be alone than chase around people who don't give two fucks about you

Trying to handle an extreme and unhealthy narcissist mother isn't easy, whether you decide to stay in their lives or walk away.

If you make the decision to walk away and cut ties, the way you handle this move is important to consider. If your narcissist mother isn't abusive, being considerate and empathetic will make sure you can leave feeling good about your decision. Just keep in mind that narcissist mothers can't empathize at times, and this is because of heightened sensitivity. If you can let them down easy without exposing or confronting them, this might be the best thing to keep their self-esteem from suffering a massive blow. If abuse is present in the relationship, you have to cut the relationship quickly or in a safe way that is expedient for you.

If your Narcissist Mother Returns

Just like any person who has been involved in a relationship, your narcissist mother will probably try to contact you. They could be suspicious, angry, or hurt about why you aren't in their lives anymore depending on them and the relationship. This is understandable.

If you decided to quit talking to your parent since their actions were damaging to your well-being, their parental love isn't going to just disappear. Some people claim that narcissists don't love, but this really isn't the case. They just can't show or express their love in front of other people. Some narcissists mothers find they have loving feelings emerge when they aren't around their narcissistic supply.

They could contact you in a human manner that is caring, to gloat, or in an attempt to get you back or get something from you. Every situation, just like every individual, will be different. If at all possible, to respond to these attempted contacts, please remember to have empathy, but deliver it in a way that doesn't invite doubt, questions, or hope. Stand by what you know is best and be firm instead of being open to the things they might offer you.

If you left a relationship you had with an emotionally abusive narcissist, you might find they will get in touch with you in the future. It is advisable that you refuse contact instead of trying to reason or discuss things with them. No good will ever come from these interactions, just more harm. If they continue to contact you, and get angry, abusive, or emotional, not reacting might force them to get control of themselves and move on.

If you have taken some distance from a family member

who isn't abusive but has unhealthy narcissistic tendencies, you might take an opportunity to have a conversation. This doesn't mean you will be opening yourself up for danger but means you are trying to be present in their lives as long as they can behave themselves. If they still can't behave, you might have to figure out if you want to increase distance or continue the relationship.

No Contact

Having no contact doesn't mean it is temporary. It means leaving for good and not looking back, ever. Many people don't like the term no contact since it can easily be misconstrued as just temporarily not having communication. The bad news is narcissists are like tumors that are cancerous. They have to be removed entirely and swiftly from our lives. If this tumor isn't removed quickly, it could spread or grow into different organs. There are times when we have to cut all ties forever. This no contact phase is like rehab for the victims of narcissistic abuse. You have to have complete isolation to cleanse yourself of the narcissistic energy.

Saying goodbye is having the ability to completely let go of this toxic individual without having second thoughts or guilt. You don't have to follow them on social media, be their friend, or check in on them. Severing all ties is the only way you can move forward after being in a relationship with a narcissist mother. Having a relationship with narcissists mothers is an addiction that has been confused with love. When you are in rehab, you have to make sure you have complete isolation from all drugs to get back control of your live.

It is essential to have a support system with family and friends.

If you have had a relationship with a narcissist mother and burned bridges with friends and family, finding an online or offline abuse recovery support group will work wonders. If your insurance covers behavioral health, you need to make an appointment with a psychologist as quickly as you can after the relationship has ended. Therapy will help you with self-esteem and find the reasons why you let them abuse you. Addressing these issues is the only way to resolve them completely. Look at it as an investment in you psychological portfolio.

Chapter 10:
How to HEAL from ABUSE!

> *You were not weak*
> *You just loved*
> *Without boundaries*

Healing from Experience with a Narcissist

You know what narcissism is and you know how to deal with it. The next step is making sure that you have what is needed to truly heal from the experience. This is a process, and no one expects you to just forget the issue never happened. Working on yourself and putting yourself first is what will allow you to get over the negative consequences of your experience

Personal Self-Esteem

When someone has low self-esteem, they are more vulnerable to narcissists and other people and situations that are largely negative. In fact, narcissists look for those with low self-esteem because they know that it will make it easier to get them into their web. When you have good self-esteem, you have a healthy level of self-respect and confidence in your abilities and worth. When self-esteem is low, someone is more likely to tolerate abusive situations, not live up to their potential and become depressed.

When you have high self-esteem, you:

- Feel accepted and valued by others.

- Respect and accept yourself even when you are making mistakes.

- Recognize your positive qualities.

- Think positively concerning yourself.

- Feel worthy of being given respect and fairness by others.

- Believe in yourself and do not allow setbacks or failure stop you from pursuing your goals.

- Take pride in what you do.

Low self-esteem is characterized by:

- Putting more focus on your failures instead of your accomplishments.

- Feeling inferior or insecure.

- Feeling that others will automatically not accept you.

- Thinking negatively about yourself.

- Being very hard on yourself when it is not warranted.

- Feeling like you do not deserve good things because you think you are defective in some way.

- Doubting your ability to be successful.

Self-esteem is a part of everything that you do in life. It affects your performance at school, work and in your relationships. Low self-esteem can also stop you from living a full life since it is characterized by fear of trying new things or testing your limits.

Where Self-Esteem Comes From

Self-esteem ultimately comes from within. However, there are a number of factors that can influence it. The people around you play a role in how you see yourself. This is especially true when it comes to those close to you and those you respect. For example, if a parent is constantly critical of a child, this can damage the child's self-esteem. On the other hand, when a parent is very supportive, it helps someone to see their own value which leads to healthy self-esteem.

Every person has that inner voice that essentially tells them what to think of themselves. For some, this inner voice can be highly negative and critical. When this happens, it is easy to believe the voice and feel as though you are inferior. It is common to have negative feelings, but when you allow them to dominate, you eventually start believing them. It is important to listen to negative inner feelings, but then put them into perspective. For example, you did poorly on a test, so naturally, this is upsetting. If your inner voice tells you that you are a failure and you listen to it and do not question it, you will start to believe this, resulting in lower self-esteem.

Comparing yourself to other people is another influencer on your self-esteem. It is fine to evaluate those around you, but do not allow this to overshadow your strengths. Taking inventory of your weaknesses and strengths and focusing on what you are good at can help prevent the strengths of those around you from negatively impacting how you view yourself.

Other factors that can alter your self-esteem include:

- How people react to you.
- Illness, injury, and disability.
- Status and role in society.
- Your personal life experiences.
- Age.
- Media messages.

The media is a major influencer. For example, you see all of these seemingly perfect people in magazines and on television. It is natural for people to compare themselves and believe that what they are seeing is what they need to be. This can be especially damaging to younger children and those who already have low self-esteem. It is important to remember that every person is unique and there is no right way to look.

Improving Your Self-Esteem

The good news is that if you have low self-esteem, this does not have to remain so. There are ways to boost it and alleviate the negative thoughts and feelings from dominating your view of yourself. To get started, work on developing life skills that contribute to how you see yourself and the world around you. These include:

- Do not be afraid to identify and experience your feelings. When you push feelings down and try to ignore them, they will eventually come to the surface.

- Do not be afraid to detach yourself from negative situations and people.

- Be receptive to those around you and empathize with people.

- Think optionally and not in black and white. This allows you to solve problems better and learn new things.

- Be assertive when it is needed. Do not allow others to dictate the direction of your life.

Focus on the good things in your life and what you are good at. Low self-esteem can make it seem like you are not good enough at anything. However, when you reflect on the good, it makes it easier to remember that it does exist on days when you are feeling down.

Make a learning opportunity out of every mistake. Every person fails and makes mistakes. This is part of life. However, do not dwell on these and the negative consequences that might come with them. Spend an hour being upset because it is important to experience your emotions. However, after an hour, go into action mode and consider why the mistake or failure occurred. You will always be able to find at least one lesson. This lesson reduces the risk of mistakes and failure in the future.

Know that perfection is simply not possible. What is important is that you are putting in the effort and working to learn and get better. No person is born automatically being great at everything. Life is all about learning and working on developing the skills needed to achieve your goals.

Remember that every person has their own strengths. Imagine a world where every person is just good at everything. There would be no healthy competition, no learning, and no balance. Know your strengths and respect the strengths of others.

Know what you cannot change. For example, if you are short, you are short. You cannot change this. Once you accept what cannot be changed, you can start putting your focus on the areas of your life that can be improved.

Do not be afraid to try. You never know what you are good at until you test your limits. Have you always wanted to play soccer, but were afraid you were not good enough? Get a game going with friends or join a local team. You may be great, or you may not. Either way, you tried it, and every new thing you try expands your horizons.

Give yourself credit when you deserve it. When you do something great, be proud of yourself. It is easy to put more focus on flaws because this is just what humans do. However, when you switch your focus to the good stuff, your self-esteem will get a boost.

How to Heal from Narcissism in Your Life

Dealing with a narcissist in your life can be damaging, and it allows for a flood of negativity in your life. Once the narcissist is gone, the issues you faced do not just disappear with them. You have to take the time to heal, and this can take some time. Give yourself time and be patient with yourself. There are stages that you go through during the healing process. Learning more about these allow you to ensure that you are doing everything needed to truly heal.

During the first stage, denial is common. You do not want to believe that the narcissist in your life is a toxic person. You may make excuses for their behavior and not want to admit that they are not healthy for you. Start writing down your thoughts concerning their treatment of you. Every few days, look back at what you wrote. This allows you to identify the pattern.

The second stage involves getting to know more about narcissism. This allows you to see what they do, and it allows you to realize that they are not capable of empathy and healthy relationships. This is a hard lesson to learn, but it is imperative for you to heal.

The third stage starts the separation process. Write a letter telling the narcissist in your life that you are walking away. Be detailed about why you are walking away. Now, you will not send the letter. This is for you to find some closure as you end the relationship.

For stage four, you cut the person from your life. Once you say "goodbye" you have to remain strong. Cut off all contact and do not give into them no matter what. It is common for a narcissist to try and manipulate you back into their life. You should consider a clean break. This means that you just cut off contact and never go back. Since this requires taking your attention away from them, expect them to try and contact you. They can be very persistent. Just make sure that you never respond.

Stage five involves taking a deep look at why you started a relationship with them in the first place. What was it about the narcissist that made you want them in your life? This can help you to prevent a future experience with a narcissist. It also lets you reflect and determine if your reasons for a relationship with them are things you need to work on. For example, was your self-esteem low when you started spending time with them? If so, improving your self-esteem can prevent a future narcissist experience.

The sixth stage is all about you. You want to evaluate your weaknesses and your self-worth. Find places that need improvement and dedicate yourself to working on them. After having a narcissist in your life, it is common to be in a negative place. Take small steps to essentially recover from your experience. Every person gets through their steps in their own time. Do not rush and do not get discouraged if you are going through the motions slowly. Every day is another day without narcissism in your life.

The seventh and final stage is accepting that the situation happened and committing yourself to learning from it. Use the pain and negativity that the narcissist caused in your life to be stronger and to drive you to put the focus on self-care. You do not need anyone in your life that contributes anything negative. Remember this. You are valuable and worthy. You also want to truly forgive yourself.

How to Handle Future Narcissism in Your Life

This ultimately comes down to knowing your worth and putting up your boundaries with any narcissist you might meet in the future. With improved self-esteem and knowing how to approach those who are narcissistic, you can better avoid falling into their web and having your life filled with their negativity.

First and foremost, make a pact with yourself that you will never allow another narcissist to take control of you. You are valuable, and your worth is determined by you and not them. They can quickly worm their way into your life because they are charming. It is easy not to believe a narcissist is a narcissist at first. They can be initially nice, or at least seem that way based on their actions and their desire to control and manipulate you.

Consider your past experience with a narcissist. Do you remember how the relationship began? Look for similar patterns with any new person in your life whom you think might be a narcissist. Remembering history is one of the best ways to prevent issues from your past from repeating themselves. It can be hard to spot the signs at first, so be diligent and do not discount your feelings if you think another narcissist has entered your life.

Go to your support system and people you trust. Ask their opinion about the person you think might be a narcissist. In many cases, when you are getting close to someone, it can be difficult to see their flaws. However, your close friends and family are on the outside looking it and can pick up on issues faster and easier than you can. Just remember that if their opinions are negative, do not get defensive. They care about you and want to ensure that you are surrounded by good people.

Practice regular self-care. When you are taking care of yourself and putting yourself first, you are less vulnerable to the charms and manipulations of a narcissist. There are numerous ways to practice self-care. You can choose one or several methods depending on your needs and what you want. The following are common self-care methods to consider:

• Make your schedule simpler so that you can put more focus on the activities that make you happy and alleviate your stress.

• Take a warm bath, and use this time to read a book, listen to your favorite songs, or just kick back. Make sure the atmosphere is relaxing and that this is time just for you. Turn off your phone and eliminate any distractions.

• Get some physical activity since this will help to boost your physical, mental, and emotional health. It is a good way to blow off some steam. Any type of physical activity that you enjoy will provide you with benefits.

• Create a list of what you are grateful for. A narcissist can take away your joy, so sometimes you need to remind yourself of the things in your life that are great.

• Find a mentor that can aid you in getting to know yourself and guide you through difficult times. This can be a religious leader, a therapist, or any person in this realm.

• Take a day to unplug from everything. Turn off all electronics and go back to a simpler time. Take a walk or a nap, enjoy favorite foods, play games with friends, or anything else that does not require electronics.

- Try something new. Have you been wanting to start painting or write a book? Is there a type of cuisine you have not tried before? As long as it is something new to you, do it. This gets you out of your comfort zone and expands your horizons.

- Go dancing. Just like physical activity, dancing can alleviate stress, and it contributes to greater well-being. Hit a club with friends or crank up some tunes in your living room and dance it out.

- Get out in nature. Nature indeed has a way to make you feel calmer and more relaxed. It is also quiet and allows you to engage in self-reflection. A quick walk or hike is a great place to start.

- Learn how to meditate. Even just five minutes of meditation per day can help to keep you grounded and it makes it easier to deal with stressors.

- Start a journal to keep track of your thoughts and feelings.

- Eliminate the clutter in your living space. When your home is more organized and clean, this helps to make you calmer. Clutter naturally induces feelings of stress.

- Make sure to get adequate sleep. Get yourself on a regular sleeping schedule and stick to it. If you want to take a nap during the day, keep it to an hour or less so that it does not interfere with your ability to sleep at night.

Conclusion

The truth will always come out. Don't miss it when it does.

Narcissism is affecting more and more people in the world today. If narcissism was a rare occurrence in the past, incidences are on a steady and dangerous rise right now. What makes this rise faster than it should is social media.

It has increased your chances of meeting with a narcissist significantly. Be ready to handle any challenge they might throw at you. If you must live with a narcissist, it is imperative that you take appropriate steps to secure your safety. Be prepared for all of his outbursts of rage.

Narcissists can be extremely charming and are master manipulators. So be ready and vigilant for any scam they might try to pull over you. It is easy to lapse into a narcissistic personality nowadays. Taking a few selfies or making a few self-appraising comments on social media need not necessarily turn you into a modern-day

Narcissus. However, it would be best for your interests if you kept such interactions to a bare minimum.

No one is going to assess your worth by going through your Facebook or Twitter profile. Keep your emotions intact. Do not drift off into a stage where you don't care about anyone but yourself. Indulging in luxuries may be a necessary addition to certain lifestyles. Make sure that you always value people and relationships above all things material.

Made in the USA
Middletown, DE
22 August 2020